MW00805313

LAROUSSE
COCKTAILS

LAROUSSE COCKTAILS

THE ULTIMATE EXPERT GUIDE WITH MORE THAN 200 RECIPES

hamlyn

CONTENTS

STARTING OUT

Cocktails are extremely popular today and anyone can have a go at being a bartender, but mixology remains an art. To avoid making mistakes, familiarize yourself with the techniques and equipment needed to enter this world. Immerse yourself in these recipes, from the most classic to the most innovative. Follow the advice of our acclaimed writers, bartenders and mixologists, and you too can become a true cocktail expert.

EQUIPMENT

There are two types of cocktail shaker. The recipes in this book have been made using a Boston shaker, consisting of two cups. Ingredients are poured into the lower part (the smaller cup) and ice cubes placed in the upper part (the larger cup made of stainless steel). In most of the recipes, after shaking vigorously, the mixture needs to be strained through a sieve to extract the ice cubes and other solid material. If you own a shaker with a built-in strainer, it is even easier, as you simply put the ingredients and ice cubes in a single cup, then close it before shaking briskly and filtering through the strainer built into the lid. Whichever method you use, avoid shaking the mix for too long. Shaking for more than 10 seconds runs the risk of the ice breaking up and starting to melt, thereby diluting the cocktail.

INGREDIENTS

Most of the different spirits used in this book are sold in supermarkets or liquor stores but any that you are unable to find in store can be purchased online. For the more unusual spirits you will find a website at the end of relevant recipe, so you can be confident of tracking them down. Flavoured vodkas and infused rums can be bought ready-prepared, but you can also easily make them yourself. For example, to make a flavoured vodka, simply put pieces of fruit in a bottle of plain vodka and let it macerate for at least 8–10 days before straining. Advice appears throughout this book on how to make these blends. Vegetable and fruit juices are always better freshly made so it's worth preparing them yourself using a juice extractor (if you have one) or an ordinary liquidizer. It is also important to use the finest quality ingredients that have first been well chilled. Remember that your cocktail can only be as good as the ingredients that go into making it.

BAR EQUIPMENT

Having the right equipment is very important.
Among the multitude of utensils available today for making cocktails, some are and always will be essential.

1 – Shaker: regarded by cocktail lovers as the bartender's most iconic tool, its purpose is to mix a cocktail quickly without diluting it too much in order to preserve its flavour and balance. Shakers are available in different designs and under different names, depending on their place of origin, such as the continental or the Boston shaker. Used to 'shake' cocktails made with fruit juices, syrups, dairy products and eggs, or even solid ingredients such as vegetables, herbs and spices.

Different types of shaker:
The 'three-piece' shaker, preferred by amateur bartenders, consists of a main cup with a lid and cap. It also has the advantage of a strainer built into the lid.
The Boston shaker from the United States consists of two cups, one large and one smaller, that fit together. The smaller one can be made of glass.
The continental shaker, similar to its American counterpart, has two metal cups that fit together for mixing ice and cocktail.

3 – Measure: known universally as a jigger, this small bar utensil allows you to measure the exact amount of alcohol needed to add to a cocktail every time. Very popular for many years with the international bartender community, it was only much later that the jigger made a breakthrough in France, coinciding with the revival of the cocktail's popularity at the beginning of the 2000s. In fact, it had been a French tradition that each bartender must master the ability to pour the perfect measure without using any utensil. However, the new generation of bartenders recognized the jigger as a means of combining style with perfection, by alternating the use of conical Japanese jiggers with cylindrical English ones. Measures vary according to the type chosen, but the most common have capacities of 60ml/30ml (2oz/1oz) and 50ml/25ml (1⅔oz/⅔oz).

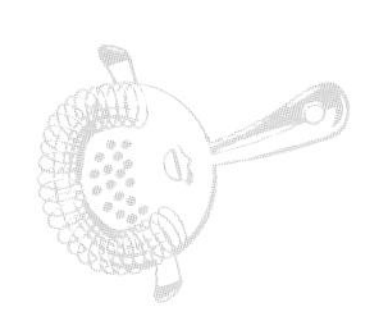

2 – Strainer: if you use the Boston shaker or continental shaker, it is necessary to filter the mixture by passing it through a strainer. You can also strain your cocktail twice, in which case you will need a second strainer that looks like a miniature conical sieve. Depending on the type of shaker, it is mostly used in conjunction with a spring-loaded strainer to filter the liquid into the glass, as well as a fine-mesh, conical style strainer to catch any small ice crystals and fruit pulp.

4 – Bar spoon: the so-called bar spoon is a very versatile implement that is much appreciated by bartenders. It can vary in size and shape, but also in unit of measure. Its main purpose is to mix or stir cocktails made in a mixing glass or directly in a glass. It can also be used as a measure since most bar spoons have a capacity of a standard teaspoon (5ml). You can use a barspoon to create the layers in cocktails such as the B52. Certain Japanese models have a spoon with a trident at the other end for piercing fruit, while other, more standard ones, are equipped with a pestle to crush sugar cubes. The spoon is also used to cool a mixing glass with ice cubes. Just remember to remove the surplus water after chilling the glass!

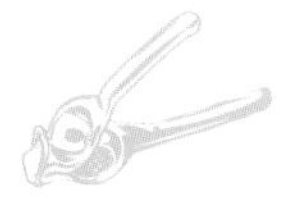

5 – Citrus press: a juicer that allows you to squeeze the juice very rapidly from citrus fruits, with a little dexterity on your part, while also trapping the pips.

BAR EQUIPMENT

6 – Mixing glass: made of glass or stainless steel, this is used to mix cocktails while cooling them and simultaneously providing controlled dilution. It is much easier to judge the liquid level in a mixing glass made of glass than in a silver or stainless steel shaker. A mixing glass is always used with a bar spoon and cocktail strainer or julep strainer. Juices, dairy products or even syrups are never mixed in a mixing glass, which is usually reserved for cocktails made entirely from spirits that require special attention during preparation.

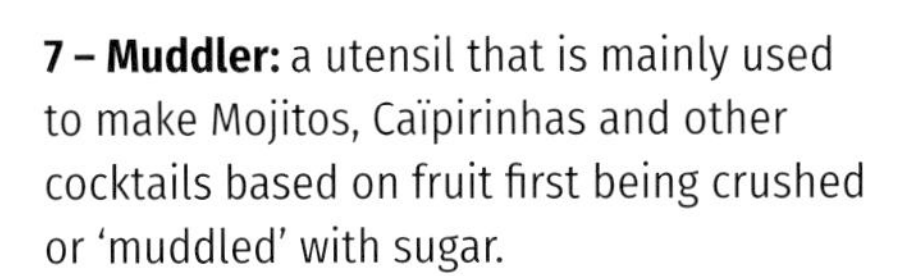

7 – Muddler: a utensil that is mainly used to make Mojitos, Caïpirinhas and other cocktails based on fruit first being crushed or 'muddled' with sugar.

8 – Tongs: for reasons of hygiene, it is worth equipping yourself with a pair of tongs for picking up pieces of fruit and ice.

9 – Glassware: choosing the correct serving glass is also important when making cocktails (*see* pages 54–55). Short drinks are cocktails with a volume of between 120ml (4oz) and 150ml (5oz), while long drinks are between 250ml (9oz) and 300ml (10oz). A short drink is served dry, that is to say without ice, while for a long drink the glass is usually filled with ice cubes. The Old Fashioned is an exception as it is served over ice.

Cocktails are made in a variety of ways. They can be blended using a liquidizer, made in a shaker, mixed directly in the glass or in a mixing glass. The mixing glass is a reminder of James Bond, who likes his Vesper martini made not with a spoon but in a shaker. As he says: 'shaken, not stirred'.

RUM

THE cocktails

RUM & CACHAÇA

Rum was first made by distilling sugar cane juice that was produced by simply grinding the cane. Today, however, more than 90 per cent of global rum production uses molasses, the thick, viscous residue remaining after the cane has been refined into brown sugar. With a much lower price when compared with cane sugar juice, a longer shelf life and a less complex distillation process, molasses represent the ideal raw material for major rum manufacturers. The Brazilian equivalent is cachaça which, to qualify as such, has to be made from pure cane juice, distilled at low temperature and bottled immediately afterwards.

In the collective imagination, spirits made from sugar cane, such as rum and cachaça, are often associated with cocktails, and from their very start inspired devotees to mix them.

Sir Francis Drake, nicknamed *El Draque* (the dragon) by the Spanish and renowned for his legendary exploits with the English fleet in the 16th century, was also one of the first people to taste a blend of cane spirits, created by his cousin, Richard Drake. Made from tafia (molasses rum), cane sugar, *hierba buena* (a wild mint that grows at the foot of sugar cane) and lime, this cocktail was a first attempt at mixing the celebrated mojito.

Just over a century later, an English naval officer named Edward Vernon and nicknamed 'Old Grog' due to the ancient moth-eaten grogram jacket he wore, decided to control the sailors' consumption of rum in an attempt to reduce alcoholism in their ranks. Despite the medicinal benefits of rum being recognized at that time, it did not make the sailors any less drunk and dangerous under its influence. To reduce the quantity consumed each day, Edward Vernon forced his crew to cut the rum with water, thereby creating what would later become, with a few minor improvements, Grog.

As can be seen, sugar cane juice distilled into rum has always sparked interest whether drunk neat or used in making cocktails. Today, it is one of the most enjoyed and frequently consumed spirits in the world.

RUM

CLASSIC MOJITO

MAKES 1

10 fresh mint leaves
½ lime, diced
3 tsp brown sugar
40ml (1⅓oz) Cuban rum
ice cubes
40ml (1⅓oz) soda water
dash of Angostura® Bitters

TO DECORATE

1 mint sprig
slice of lime

Place the mint leaves, lime and brown sugar in a tumbler and muddle them together, then add the rum. Fill with ice cubes and finally add the soda water. Mix everything together and then add the Angostura bitters. Serve with a straw and decorate with a mint sprig and a slice of lime.

RUM

CAÏPIRINHA

MAKES 1

½ lime, diced
1 tbsp brown sugar
ice cubes or crushed ice
60ml (2oz) cachaça

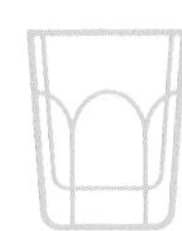

Place the lime and brown sugar in an Old-Fashioned cocktail glass. Rotate the glass so the mixture settles on the inner wall of it. Fill the glass with ice cubes or crushed ice and lastly add the cachaça. Mix with a bar spoon.

Note

Caïpirinha is *the* national cocktail of Brazil and enjoys global fame. A symbol of celebration and music, it brings people together through a spirit that was previously unknown: cachaça!

BONFIM DA

RUM

MARTINIQUE PUNCH

MAKES 4.5 LITRES (152OZ)

1.5 litres (51oz) Martinique rum
450ml (16oz) guava juice
450ml (16oz) pineapple juice
450ml (16oz) orange juice
450ml (16oz) passion fruit juice
450ml (16oz) vanilla syrup
ice cubes
1 lemon
1 orange
½ pineapple
1 passion fruit
1 stick of lemongrass
1 rosemary sprig

Pour all the liquid ingredients into a cocktail fountain or large bowl. Mix, then add some ice cubes. Cut the lemon and orange into slices and the pineapple into quarters. Add them to the cocktail fountain or bowl with the passion fruit pulp, lemongrass and rosemary and mix again.

INDIAN PUNCH

MAKES 4.5 LITRES (152OZ)

1.5 litres (51oz) white rum
1.35 litres (46oz) freshly squeezed lime juice
900ml (30oz) hibiscus syrup
450ml (16oz) vanilla syrup
ice cubes
1 lime
5 dried hibiscus flowers

Pour all the liquid ingredients into a cocktail fountain or large bowl. Mix, then add some ice cubes. Cut the lime into slices and add them to the cocktail fountain or bowl with the hibiscus flowers.

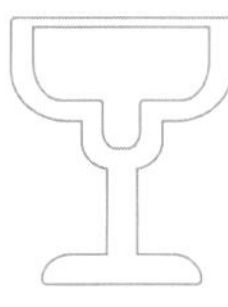

RUM

MAI TAÏ

MAKES 4.5 LITRES (152OZ)

1.5 litres (51oz) white rum
450ml (16oz) triple sec
1.35 litres (46oz) freshly squeezed lime juice
900ml (30oz) orgeat (almond) syrup
ice cubes
1 lime

Pour all the liquid ingredients into a cocktail fountain or large bowl. Mix, then add some ice cubes. Cut the lime into slices, add them to the cocktail fountain or bowl and mix again.

RUM

TI'PUNCH

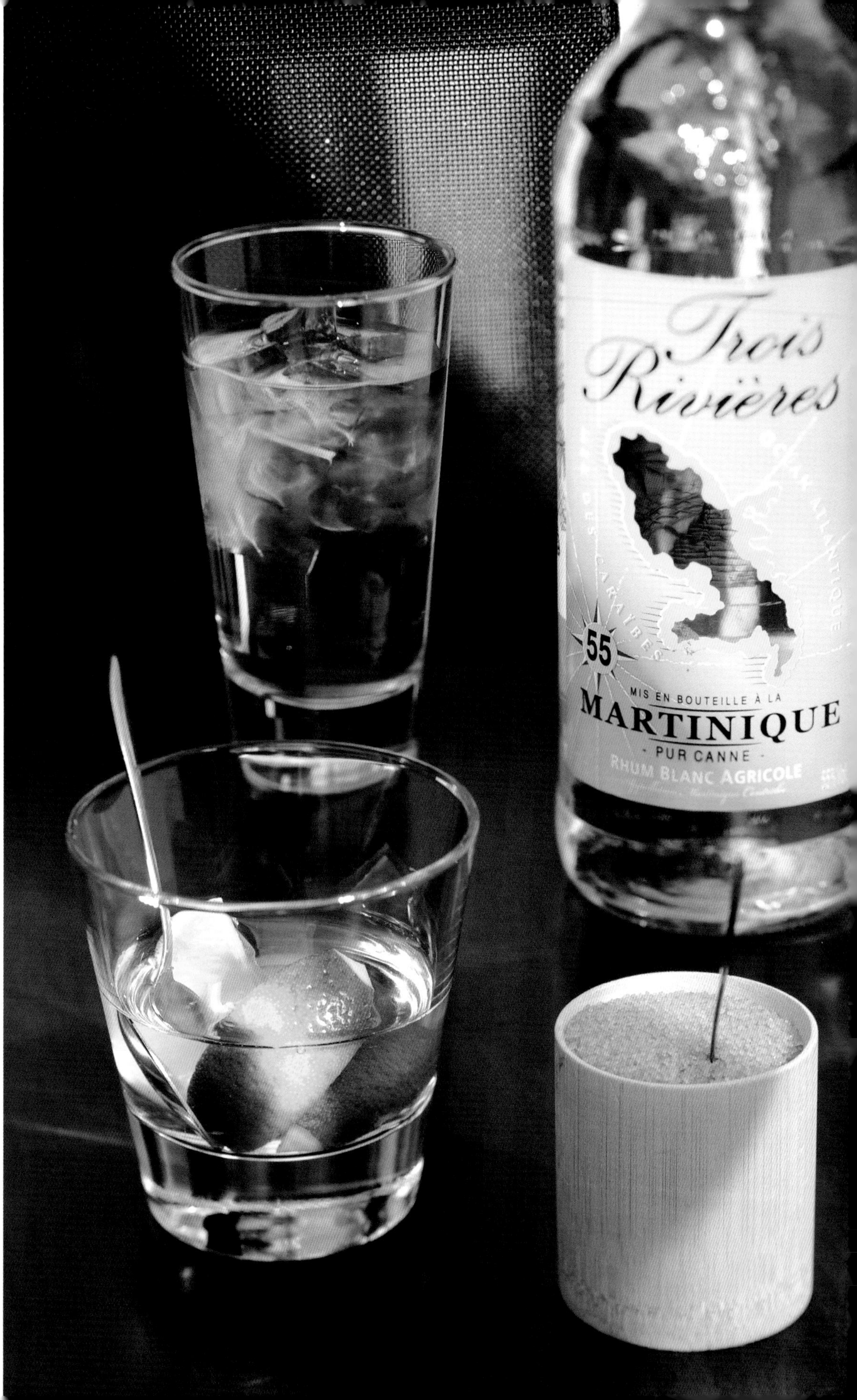

A Martinique institution, Ti'Punch is made using only locally made rum with at least 50% ABV. This cocktail is best drunk without ice, accompanied by a glass of well-chilled water.

MAKES 1

10ml (2 tsp) sugar cane syrup (or 1 tsp icing sugar)
¼ lime
40ml (1⅓oz) Martinique *rhum agricole* with 50% ABV (for example, Trois Rivières)

Put the sugar cane syrup (or icing sugar) in an Old-Fashioned glass and then add the juice from the lime quarter, squeezing it in between two fingers. Pour in the rum. Serve with a glass of well-chilled water.

RUM

VINTAGE GROG

MAKES 1

50ml (1⅔oz) freshly squeezed lemon juice
20ml (⅔oz) acacia honey
50ml (1⅔oz) hot water
1g (1 large pinch) ground cinnamon
2 drops of Angostura® Bitters
40ml (1⅓oz) amber rum
strip of lemon zest studded with whole cloves

Heat all the ingredients, except the lemon zest, in a saucepan over a low heat. Stir, pour into a heatproof glass, add the lemon zest studded with whole cloves and serve.

RUM

PIÑA COLADA

The Piña Colada was invented in Puerto Rico between 1950 and 1960 and its name translates as 'overripe pineapple'. The cocktail can also can be served in a hollowed-out pineapple shell. Coconut pulp is added but not coconut cream.

MAKES 1

30ml (1oz) coconut milk
70ml ($2\frac{1}{3}$oz) pineapple juice
40ml ($1\frac{1}{3}$oz) white *rhum agricole*
ice cubes

TO DECORATE

coconut powder (optional)
1 small piece of fresh pineapple
1 maraschino cherry

Pour the coconut milk, pineapple juice and rum into a liquidizer. Add several ice cubes and blend thoroughly until smooth. Pour into a glass tumbler, frosted if wished, with coconut powder. Decorate with a piece of fresh pineapple and a maraschino cherry.

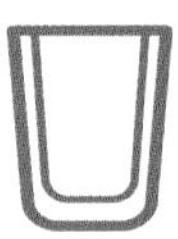

MAKES 1

2 feijoa, cut into pieces
20ml ($\frac{2}{3}$oz) grapefruit juice
20ml ($\frac{2}{3}$oz) pineapple juice
40ml ($1\frac{1}{3}$oz) guava juice
60ml (2oz) cachaça
ice cubes

Put the feijoa, grapefruit juice, pineapple juice, guava juice and cachaça into a liquidizer. Blend for 20 seconds and then pour into a glass filled with ice cubes. Serve the cocktail accompanied with a selection of exotic fruits.

GRANDE PASSION

MAKES 1

40ml (1⅓oz) cachaça, infused with vanilla and cinnamon (*see* Note)
30ml (1oz) almond milk
20ml (⅔oz) grenadine liqueur
50ml (1⅔oz) pineapple juice
30ml (1oz) mango juice
ice cubes and crushed ice

Pour the vanilla- and cinnamon-infused cachaça, the almond milk, grenadine liqueur, pineapple juice and mango juice into a cocktail shaker. Fill the shaker with ice cubes, close it, and then shake vigorously for 5–10 seconds. Strain and pour the mixture into a glass filled with crushed ice.

Note

To make 700ml (24oz) of cachaça infused with vanilla and cinnamon, you will need 700ml (24oz) cachaça, 2 vanilla pods and 3 cinnamon sticks. Pour the cachaça into a saucepan. Split the vanilla pods and add them to the saucepan with the cinnamon sticks. Stir over the heat for a few minutes until the liquid comes to the boil, then remove the saucepan from the heat and pour the mixture into a hermetically sealed jar. Leave to infuse for 48 hours.

AFRICAN STORY

MAKES 1

100g (½ cup) pineapple, peeled and cored
10ml (2 tsp) vanilla liqueur
40ml (1⅓oz) white *rhum agricole*
20ml (⅔oz) bissap (hibiscus) syrup
ice cubes

TO DECORATE

1 vanilla pod

In a cocktail shaker, muddle the pineapple with the vanilla liqueur. Add the white rum and bissap syrup. Fill the shaker with ice, close it, and shake vigorously for 5–10 seconds. Strain twice through a sieve, then through a mini conical strainer into a cocktail glass. Decorate with a vanilla pod.

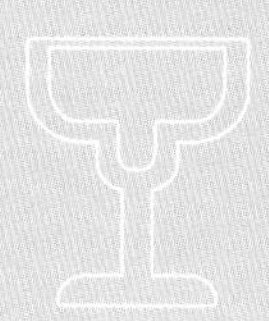

RUM

STRAWBERRY-INFUSED RUM

MAKES 1 LITRE (34OZ)

800ml (28oz) white *rhum agricole* (50% ABV)
150ml (5oz) sugar cane syrup
3 tbsp brown sugar
6 strawberries

Pour the rum and sugar cane syrup into a glass bottle and add the brown sugar. Cut the strawberries in half and add them to the bottle. Leave to macerate for 1 week, making sure you stir the mixture frequently.

Note

After a few days the strawberries will become white and the rum garnet coloured, so you may prefer to replace the strawberries with fresh ones before serving.

RUM

CARAMELITO MOJITO

MAKES 1

10 mint leaves
½ lime, diced
4 cubes of pineapple
10ml (2 tsp) liquid caramel, plus extra for drizzling
40ml (1⅓oz) Cuban rum
crushed ice
40ml (1⅓oz) Canada Dry® ginger ale

TO DECORATE

1 mint sprig
pineapple chunks threaded onto a cocktail stick

Begin by putting the mint leaves, lime, pineapple cubes and caramel in a tumbler. Muddle everything together, then add the rum. Fill the glass with crushed ice and top up with the ginger ale. Mix well and decorate your mojito with a mint sprig. Sit the cocktail stick threaded with 3 pineapple chunks on top of the glass and drizzle with extra caramel liquid.

RUM

SPICED RUM

MAKES 1

8 large mint leaves
8 large Thai basil leaves
¾ lime, diced
crushed ice
50ml (1⅔oz) rum infused with currants and basil (*see* Note)
30ml (1oz) masala spice mix (*see* Note)
Ginger ale, eg Schweppes®, to top up

Muddle the mint leaves, basil leaves and lime in a tumbler. Fill the glass with crushed ice and add the infused rum and masala mix. Top up with ginger ale and mix by stirring with a bar spoon.

Note

To prepare 700ml (24oz) **rum infused with currants and basil**, you will need 1 bottle of rum, 100g (⅔ cup) currants and 20 Thai basil leaves. Put the currants and Thai basil in a 1 litre (1¾ pint) bottle. Heat the rum in a saucepan over a low heat until it is warm (without letting it boil), then pour it into the bottle. Seal the bottle, shake vigorously and leave to infuse for 5 days at room temperature.

For 200ml (7oz) **masala mix**, put 100ml (3½oz) mango smoothie, 100ml (3½oz) passion fruit smoothie and ½g (1 large pinch) garam masala in a bottle. Seal the bottle tightly and shake vigorously, then chill in the refrigerator (up to a maximum of 3 days) until ready to serve.

RUM

FLASH BACK

MAKES 4

4–5 tonka beans
160ml ($5^1/_4$oz) old rum
380ml (13oz) cold vanilla tea
ice cubes
120ml (4oz) elderflower liqueur (St-Germain)
pulp of 2 passion fruit

Infuse the tonka beans in the old rum for 3 days and then strain. Make the vanilla tea, leave it to cool and keep chilled until needed. Half-fill a cocktail shaker with ice cubes, pour in the rum, liqueur and cold tea and add the passion fruit pulp. Shake vigorously, strain into 4 glasses and serve with a straw.

LUCKY TIME

MAKES 4

ice cubes or crushed ice
4 dates
280ml ($9^1/_2$oz) pear juice
280ml ($9^1/_2$oz) almond milk
80ml ($2^2/_3$oz) ginger syrup
160ml ($5^1/_4$oz) amber rum

Half-fill a liquidizer with ice. Halve the dates, remove their stones and add to the liquidizer with the pear juice, almond milk, ginger syrup and rum. Blend for about 10 seconds and then serve.

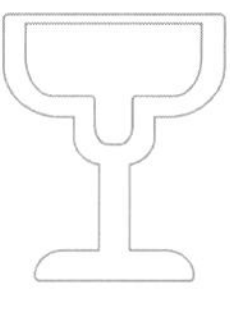

RUM

BAJAN COOLER

In 1910, a total eclipse of the sun, combined with the passage of Halley's comet, led to the creation of 'Eclipse' rum, the unparalled depth and complexity of which perfectly embodies rum produced in Barbados.

MAKES 1

20ml (2⁄3oz) passion fruit purée (or strained pulp of 1⁄2 passion fruit)
50ml (1 2⁄3oz) amber Barbados rum (Mount Gay® Eclipse)
ice cubes or crushed ice
100ml (3 1⁄2oz) ginger beer

TO DECORATE

1 mint sprig

Pour the passion fruit purée (or strained pulp of 1⁄2 passion fruit) and the rum into a cocktail shaker filled with ice. Close the shaker and shake vigorously. Pour into a tumbler filled with ice cubes or crushed ice and top up with the ginger beer. Decorate with a mint sprig.

RUM

RUMBULLION 1881

MAKES 4.5 LITRES (152OZ)

1.5 litres (51oz) Martinique rum
900ml (30oz) kiwi juice
900ml (30oz) passion fruit juice
900ml (30oz) pineapple juice
ice cubes
1 kiwi fruit
½ pineapple
2 passion fruit

Pour all the liquid ingredients into a cocktail fountain or large bowl. Mix, then add some ice cubes. Peel and slice the kiwi fruit and cut the pineapple into quarters. Add them to the cocktail fountain or bowl with the pulp from the passion fruit and mix again.

Cold

RUM

CITRUS-INFUSED RUM

MAKES 1 LITRE (34OZ)

750ml (27oz) *rhum agricole* (50% ABV)
150ml (5oz) sugar cane syrup
3 tbsp brown sugar
zest of 1 orange
zest of 1 lemon
zest of ½ pomelo

Pour the rum and sugar syrup into a bottle and add the brown sugar. Using a zester or vegetable peeler, shave the zest from the citrus fruits and add to the bottle. Leave to macerate for 1 week, making sure to stir the mixture frequently.

APPLE & CINNAMON-INFUSED RUM

MAKES 1 LITRE (34OZ)

750ml (25oz) *rhum agricole* (50% ABV)
150ml (5oz) sugar cane syrup
3 tbsp brown sugar
2–3 apples
4 cinnamon sticks

Pour the rum and sugar syrup into a bottle and add the brown sugar. Cut the apples into quarters, taking care to remove all the seeds. Place the apple quarters and cinnamon sticks in the bottle. Leave to macerate for 1 week. If the flavour of the cinnamon becomes too strong, remove the sticks from the bottle and make sure to stir the mixture frequently.

RUM

RED BERRIES MOJITO

MAKES 1

10 mint leaves
½ lime, diced
10ml (2 tsp) sugar syrup
40ml (1⅓oz) Cuban rum
crushed ice
40ml (1⅓oz) red berry coulis
(or puréed mixed berries)
40ml (1⅓oz) soda water

TO DECORATE

mixed berries such as raspberries
and blueberries

Begin by putting the mint leaves, lime and sugar syrup in a tumbler. Muddle everything together and then add the rum. Fill the glass with crushed ice and finish by adding the coulis and soda water. Mix well, then serve the mojito with a straw and decorate with a cocktail stick threaded with mixed berries.

THIS

RUM

SNOWFLAKE

Pour the agave syrup, lychee syrup, coconut milk and cachaça into a cocktail shaker. Fill the shaker with ice cubes, close it and shake vigorously. Strain the mixture through a sieve and then pour into a martini glass to serve.

MAKES 1

10ml (2 tsp) agave syrup
10ml (2 tsp) lychee syrup
20ml (⅔oz) coconut milk
40ml (1⅓oz) cachaça
ice cubes

SMILE

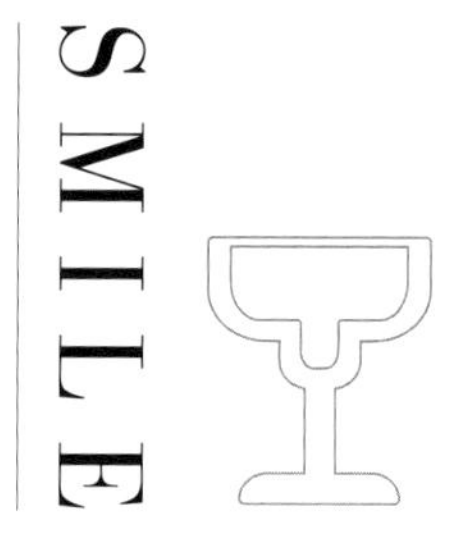

MAKES 1

ice cubes
50ml (1⅔oz) pineapple juice
40ml (1⅓oz) mango nectar
1 passion fruit
20ml (⅔oz) ginger syrup
50ml (1⅔oz) rum
10ml (2 tsp) vanilla liqueur

Half-fill a liquidizer with ice cubes and add the pineapple juice and mango nectar. Cut the passion fruit in half and, using a teaspoon, scoop out the pulp into the liquidizer. Add the ginger syrup, rum and vanilla liqueur. Blend for about 10 seconds. Pour into a fancy glass and serve with a straw.

RUM

ZOMBIE

MAKES 4.5 LITRES (152OZ)

1 litre (34oz) white rum
900ml (30oz) amber rum
900ml (30oz) passion fruit juice
900ml (30oz) pineapple juice
450ml (16oz) apricot liqueur
350ml (12oz) grenadine syrup
ice cubes
½ pineapple
3 passion fruit

Pour all the liquid ingredients into a cocktail fountain or large bowl. Mix, then add some ice cubes. Cut the pineapple into quarters and add to the cocktail fountain or bowl with the pulp from the passion fruit.

For extra wow factor for your guests, scoop the pulp out of half a passion fruit and fill the half-shell with rum. Flambé the rum and serve alongside the cocktail.

RUM

MARCEL RUM

MAKES 1

60ml (2oz) freshly squeezed lemon juice
120ml (4oz) freshly squeezed orange juice
20ml (2/3oz) sugar syrup
60ml (2oz) white Antilles rum
2g (1/4 tsp) ground cinnamon

Warm the lemon juice, orange juice, sugar syrup and rum over a gentle heat. Add the cinnamon, remove from the heat and serve.

CHESTNUT RUM TEA

MAKES 1

120ml (4oz) milk
2 tsp chestnut purée
70ml (2 1/3oz) black tea
40ml (1 1/3oz) 3-year-old Cuban rum
20ml (2/3oz) crème de châtaigne liqueur (Combier®)

TO DECORATE

pieces of *marrons glacés*

Put the milk and chestnut purée in a whipped cream siphon and fit with two gas cartridges. Rotate the siphon up and down from top to bottom in order to mix the contents well and circulate the gas. Refrigerate for 24 hours. Make the black tea, add the rum and crème de châtaigne liqueur and pour into a glass. Dispense the milk foam from the siphon on top and decorate with pieces of *marrons glacés*.

RUM

BASIL & CHERRY-INFUSED RUM

MAKES 1 LITRE (34OZ)

750ml (25oz) *rhum agricole* (50% ABV)
150ml (5oz) sugar cane syrup
2 tsp brown sugar
25g (1oz) cherries
10 basil leaves
1 drop of edible large green basil essential oil (optional)

Pour the rum, sugar cane syrup and brown sugar into a cocktail fountain or Mason jar. Wash and dry the cherries and basil leaves, remove the cherry stalks, and add both to the fountain or jar. Add the drop of essential oil (if using) and stir. Leave to macerate for 3 weeks, making sure to stir the mixture frequently. Strain before serving.

Enjoy neat, over ice or with a little soda water.

Glassware

Both in terms of the way a cocktail looks and how it is made, the type of glass in which it is served in is very important. Each cocktail will have its own adapted size and shape of glass. Whereas Martini glasses are used for drinks served without ice, such as a Cosmopolitan and so called 'short drinks', champagne flutes are perfect for sparkling cocktails. Small shot glasses normally reserved exclusively for shooters, can also work well for other small cocktails or for enjoying spirits neat. For cocktails served with crushed ice, it is better to use impressive glasses such as those designed for serving toddies. As their name suggests, wine glasses have been designed for wine but they may also be suitable for fruity cocktails like sangria or punch.

A Martini glass is recommended for serving a short drink 'straight up', 'chilled' and quite often 'frozen'. It holds around 200ml (7oz).

Holding around 250ml (9oz), this glass is for serving wines. It can also be used for some cocktails such as a Spritz.

HIGHBALL GLASS

This style of class is also known as a Collins glass or even a large tumbler. The Highball Glass is used for cocktails such as Gin Fizz. It holds around 350ml (12oz).

ROCKS GLASS

This type of glass is also called an Old Fashioned or even a small tumbler. Cocktails such as Caïpirinha, Black Russian and Gimlet are served in it. It holds around 300ml (10oz).

CHAMPAGNE FLUTE

A flute is for champagne-based cocktails, except when they are served with ice cubes where a highball glass is used. It holds around 180ml (6oz).

TASTING GLASS

The shape of this glass makes it ideal for assessing the quality of spirits. As a rule, a tasting glass is rarely used for serving cocktails. It holds around 120ml (4 oz).

SHOT GLASS

Its capacity is approximately 60ml (2oz) and is ideal for drinking a cocktail in one mouthful. The shot glass is traditionally used to consume tequila and vodka, served neat.

TODDY GLASS

This is used for serving hot cocktails since it is specially made to withstand thermal shock when boiling water is poured into it. It holds around 250ml (9oz).

RUM

PINK MOJITO

MAKES 1

10 mint leaves
½ lime, diced
10ml (2 tsp) rose syrup
40ml (1⅓oz) Cuban rum
crushed ice
20ml (⅔oz) colourless peach liqueur (Peachtree®)
40ml (1⅓oz) soda water

TO DECORATE

1 mint sprig
1 peach quarter

Put the mint leaves, lime and rose syrup in a tumbler. Muddle them together and then add the rum. Fill the glass with crushed ice and finish by adding the peach liqueur and soda water. Mix everything together and then decorate your mojito with a mint sprig and peach quarter. Serve with a straw.

RUM

EASTERN PRALINETTE

Halve the dates and remove the stones. Place the dates in a cocktail shaker with the sugar cane syrup and add the orange juice and cachaça. Fill the shaker with ice cubes, close it and shake vigorously for 5–10 seconds. Strain through a sieve and pour the mixture into a glass. Decorate with extra whole dates.

MAKES 1

3 large dates
15ml (½oz) sugar cane syrup
15ml (½oz) orange juice
50ml (1⅔oz) cachaça
ice cubes

TO DECORATE

dates

COPACABANA

MAKES 1

6 ice cubes
40ml (1⅓oz) sweetened condensed milk
40ml (1⅓oz) acerola juice
40ml (1⅓oz) orange juice
40ml (1⅓oz) carrot juice
50ml (1⅔oz) cachaça
strip of kaffir lime zest

Put the ice cubes in a liquidizer, then pour in the condensed milk, acerola juice, orange juice, carrot juice and cachaça. Blend for 10 seconds. Pour the cocktail into a decorative glass and serve with a strip of kaffir lime zest on top.

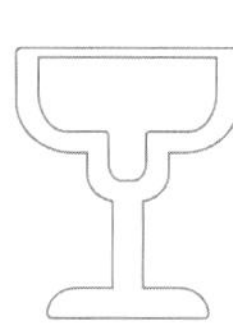

RUM

COPACABANA BEACH

MAKES 10

500ml (18oz) cachaça
200ml (7oz) freshly squeezed lime juice
100ml ($3^{1}/_{2}$oz) sugar syrup
600ml (20oz) fresh coconut water
1 lime
ice cubes
fleur de sel (optional)

Pour all the liquid ingredients into a large bowl and mix them together. Be sure to use fresh coconut water as only this has a natural iodine flavour. Cut the lime into thin slices. Add the lime slices to the bowl with some ice cubes and then serve.

Note

For a saltier flavour, half-frost the rim of your glasses with *fleur de sel*.

RUM

DRAKE MOJITO

MAKES 10

water
30 dashes of Angostura® Bitters
1 bunch mint
300ml (10oz) sugar syrup
350ml (12oz) freshly squeezed lime juice (about 9 limes)
700ml (24oz) amber rum (Havana Club® or Bacardi®)

Mix some water with the Angostura Bitters and pour the mixture into the cavities of an ice cube tray. Freeze for at least 3 hours. Lightly chop the mint and place it in a large bowl with the rest of the ingredients. Mix, then add the Angostura Bitters ice cubes. Stir and serve in Old-Fashioned glasses.

RUM

LUXURY SANGRIA

MAKES 10

1 orange
1 grapefruit
200ml (7oz) white rum
400ml (14oz) red wine
200ml (7oz) freshly squeezed orange juice
200ml (7oz) maraschino liqueur
50ml (1⅔oz) absinthe
4 cinnamon sticks
1 whole star anise
ice cubes

TO DECORATE

dried Korean chilli threads

Cut the orange and the grapefruit into slices. Put all the ingredients into a large bowl. Stir with a bar spoon to mix and then chill in the refrigerator for 3 hours. Add ice cubes just before serving decorated with dried Korean chilli threads.

RUM

STRIPED COCKTAIL

MAKES 1

20ml (⅔oz) anisette (Marie Brizard®)
20ml (⅔oz) rum
1 tsp grenadine syrup
20ml (⅔oz) sake

Pour the anisette into a glass. In another glass, mix together the rum and grenadine syrup. Add this mixture to the first glass, drizzling it over the back of a bar spoon so that the two layers remain separate. Repeat with the sake, using the spoon to create a third separate layer to the cocktail. Drink immediately.

VODKA

THE cocktails

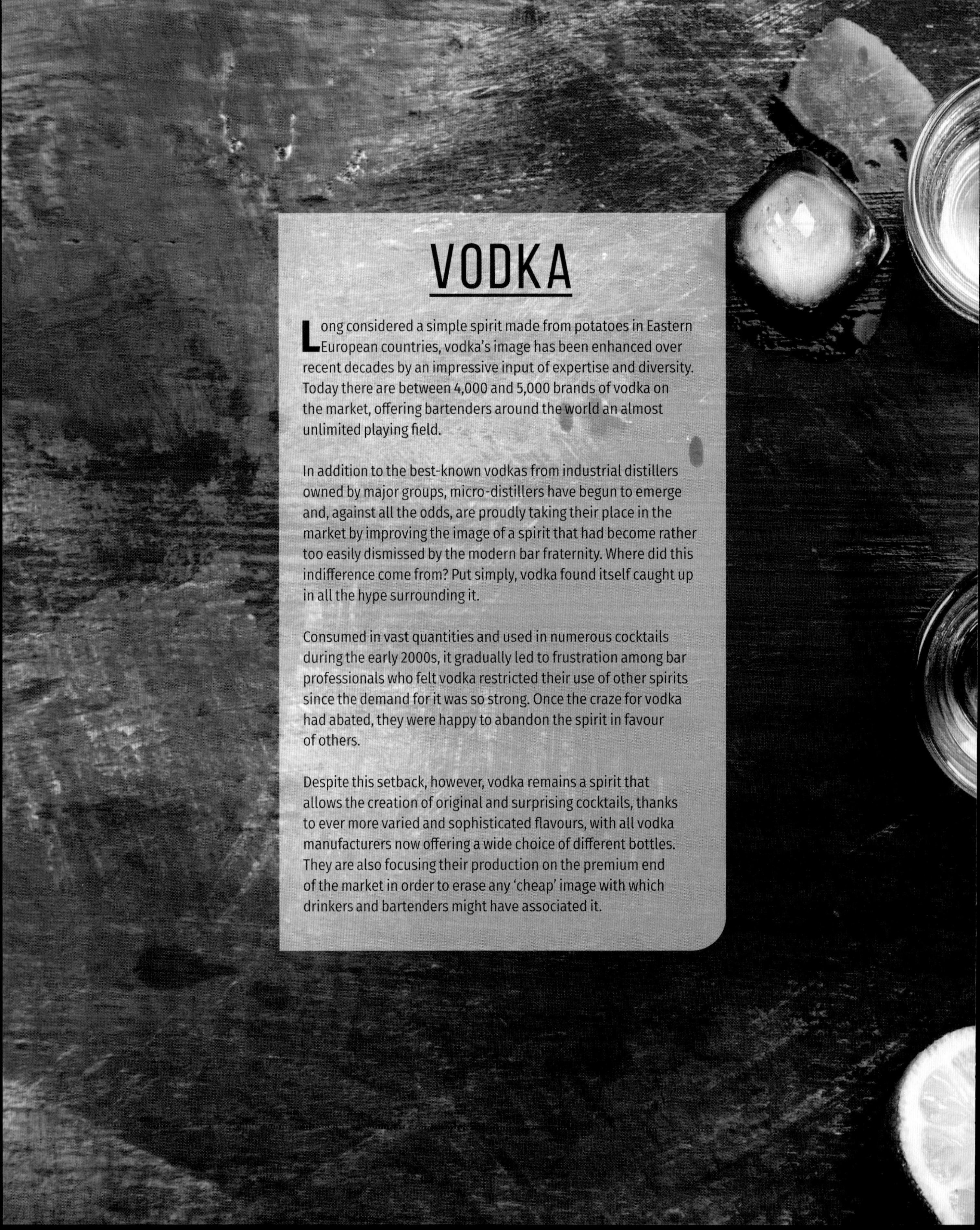

VODKA

Long considered a simple spirit made from potatoes in Eastern European countries, vodka's image has been enhanced over recent decades by an impressive input of expertise and diversity. Today there are between 4,000 and 5,000 brands of vodka on the market, offering bartenders around the world an almost unlimited playing field.

In addition to the best-known vodkas from industrial distillers owned by major groups, micro-distillers have begun to emerge and, against all the odds, are proudly taking their place in the market by improving the image of a spirit that had become rather too easily dismissed by the modern bar fraternity. Where did this indifference come from? Put simply, vodka found itself caught up in all the hype surrounding it.

Consumed in vast quantities and used in numerous cocktails during the early 2000s, it gradually led to frustration among bar professionals who felt vodka restricted their use of other spirits since the demand for it was so strong. Once the craze for vodka had abated, they were happy to abandon the spirit in favour of others.

Despite this setback, however, vodka remains a spirit that allows the creation of original and surprising cocktails, thanks to ever more varied and sophisticated flavours, with all vodka manufacturers now offering a wide choice of different bottles. They are also focusing their production on the premium end of the market in order to erase any 'cheap' image with which drinkers and bartenders might have associated it.

VODKA

COSMOPOLITAN

MAKES 10

grated zest of 1 orange and 1 lime
350ml (12oz) freshly squeezed lime juice
350ml (12oz) triple sec
200ml (7oz) cranberry juice
350ml (12oz) vodka

Grate the orange and lime zests directly into the cavities of an ice cube tray and add a little water to each. Freeze for at least 3 hours. Unmould the citrus ice cubes directly into a large bowl, then pour in the lime juice, triple sec, cranberry juice and vodka. Stir and serve in Old-Fashioned glasses.

VODKA

BLACK RUSSIAN

MAKES 4 SHOOTERS

crushed ice
100ml (3½oz) Russian Standard® vodka
60ml (2oz) coffee liqueur

Fill each shooter glass with crushed ice. Add 25ml (⅔oz plus 1 tsp) vodka, then 15ml (½oz) coffee liqueur to each and stir.

Note

To make a White Russian, follow the same recipe and simply add 10ml (2 tsp) cream to each glass before serving.

Русский
Стандарт

VODKA

MOSCOW MULE

MAKES 1

1 mint sprig
2 lime slices
ice cubes
50ml ($1^2/_3$oz) vodka
70ml ($2^1/_3$oz) ginger beer
1 drop Angostura® Bitters (optional)

TO DECORATE

1 mint sprig

Put the mint sprig and lime slices in a tumbler. Fill the glass with ice cubes, then pour in the vodka. Mix well with a bar spoon. Top up with the ginger beer, add 1 drop of Angostura Bitters, if using, and stir. Decorate with a mint sprig.

Note

This cocktail, created in 1941 in Los Angeles, was good news for vodka sales at the time and it remains the case today. Interesting fact: ginger beer is a ginger soda that is spicier than ginger ale. You can find it under the brand name of Fever Tree®.

VODKA

RUSSIAN BLUE PUNCH

MAKES 4.5 LITRES (152OZ)

1.5 litres (51oz) vodka
450ml (16oz) blue Curaçao
900ml (30oz) lychee juice
900ml (30oz) freshly squeezed lemon juice
450ml (16oz) sugar syrup
ice cubes
1 lemon
10 lychees

Pour all the liquid ingredients into a cocktail fountain or large bowl. Mix, then add some ice cubes. Cut the lemon into slices, add them to the cocktail fountain or bowl with the lychees and mix again.

VODKA

BLOODY MARY

MAKES 1

ice cubes
1 tsp celery salt
10ml (2 tsp) Worcestershire sauce
20ml (2/3oz) lemon juice
60ml (2oz) tomato juice
3 or 4 drops Tabasco®
40ml (1 1/3oz) vodka

TO DECORATE

2 cherry tomato halves
celery stick

Fill a tumbler with ice cubes, dust with the celery salt and add the Worcestershire sauce, lemon juice, tomato juice, Tabasco and vodka. Stir with a bar spoon and decorate with the cherry tomato halves threaded on a cocktail stick and a stick of celery.

Note

A Bloody Mary was the favourite cocktail of Serge Gainsbourg, who loved to drink it in the intimate bar of the Hotel Raphaël in Paris. The cocktail was created in 1921 by Ferdinand Petiot at the New York Bar (today Harry's Bar) in the Palais Garnier district of Paris.

VODKA

RUSSIAN GIMLET

A variation on a great classic, the Russian Gimlet has proved very popular at all kinds of high society receptions. Very simple to make, it's an instant hit!

MAKES 1

ice cubes
50ml (1⅔oz) Russian Standard® vodka
20ml (⅔oz) lime juice cordial

TO DECORATE

1 slice of lime

Fill a mixing glass with ice cubes and pour in the vodka and lime juice cordial. Stir, strain into a cocktail glass and decorate the rim of the glass with a slice of lime.

VODKA

SPICY MANGO MARTINI

MAKES 1

60ml (2oz) mango juice
20ml (⅔oz) mango liqueur
50ml (1⅔oz) vodka infused with a red Thai chilli (*see* Note)
3 tsp icing sugar
ice cubes

TO DECORATE

1 slice of mango
1 red Thai chilli

Pour the mango juice, mango liqueur and Thai chilli-infused vodka into a cocktail shaker and add the icing sugar. Fill the shaker with ice cubes, close it and shake vigorously for 5–10 seconds. Strain into a cocktail glass and serve without ice. Decorate with a thin slice of mango and a red Thai chilli threaded onto a cocktail stick and placed on top of the glass.

For the Thai chilli-infused vodka, slit a red Thai chilli in half lengthways and place it in a bottle of vodka. Leave to infuse for 72 hours at room temperature. Stir and filter twice, once through a strainer and once through a mini-conical sieve. Pour back into the original vodka bottle.

VODKA

S.O.T.B LAROUSSE-STYLE

S.O.T.B is the abbreviation of Sex on the Beach, a cocktail that is famous around the world. This is Larousse's version.

MAKES 1

40ml (1⅓oz) vodka
15ml (½oz) apricot liqueur
10ml (2 tsp) raspberry syrup
60ml (2oz) pineapple juice
30ml (1oz) passion fruit juice
15ml (½oz) passion fruit liqueur (Passoa®, for example)
ice cubes and crushed ice
20ml (⅔oz) strawberry purée

TO DECORATE

strawberries

Put the vodka, apricot liqueur, raspberry syrup, pineapple juice, and the passion fruit juice and liqueur in a cocktail shaker. Fill the shaker with ice cubes and shake vigorously. Pour the cocktail with the ice cubes into a glass. Add the crushed ice and finish with the strawberry purée. Decorate with a strawberry fan.

APPLE GREY

We recommend using Earl Grey to make this cocktail.

MAKES 1

¼ golden delicious apple
20ml (⅔oz) sugar cane syrup
20ml (⅔oz) green apple sour liqueur
50ml (1⅔oz) vodka infused with Earl Grey tea (*see* Note)
ice cubes

TO DECORATE

thin slices of green apple

Dice the golden delicious apple quarter, put it in a cocktail shaker with the sugar cane syrup and muddle together. Add the green apple sour liqueur and the Earl Grey tea-infused vodka. Fill the shaker with ice cubes, close it and shake energetically for 5–10 seconds. Strain twice, once using a strainer and once using a mini-conical sieve, into a Martini glass without ice. Decorate with thin slices of green apple arranged in a fan shape and held in place with a cocktail stick, for a fun flourish.

Note

Pour 1 litre (34oz) vodka into a saucepan and add 12g (½oz) Earl Grey tea leaves. Stir and then heat until the vodka comes to the boil. Pour the mixture into a bottle and leave to infuse for 8 hours. Strain before using.

VODKA

DRAGON SHADOW

For lovers of chestnut cream... It's surprising and so good in this gastronomic cocktail!

MAKES 1

ice cubes
10ml (2 tsp) cinnamon syrup
10ml (2 tsp) chestnut cream
50ml (1⅔oz) lemon-flavoured vodka

TO DECORATE

1 long strip of orange zest

Fill a cocktail shaker with ice cubes and add the cinnamon syrup, chestnut cream and lemon-flavoured vodka. Close the shaker and shake vigorously. Pour into a Martini glass without the ice cubes. Decorate with a long strip of orange zest.

BANANA VODKA

MAKES 750ML (25OZ)

600ml (20oz) vodka
120ml (4 oz) sugar cane syrup
20 banana bonbons

Pour the vodka and sugar cane syrup into a bottle. Add the banana bonbons and mix together. Leave to macerate in the refrigerator for 10 days. Strain before serving.

TONI BERRY

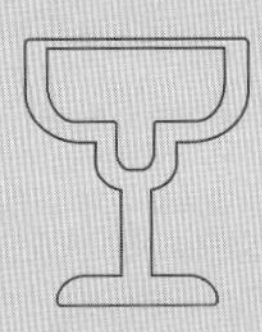

MAKES 4

ice cubes
160ml (5¼oz) vodka
80ml (2⅔oz) strawberry syrup
240ml (8½oz) cranberry juice
strips of zest from 1 lime
320ml (11oz) tonic water
(Schweppes®)

Half-fill a cocktail shaker with ice cubes and add the vodka, strawberry syrup and cranberry juice, then shake. Serve in glasses, add lime zest to each and top up with tonic water.

VODKA PEPINO

MAKES 1

1 pear
1/4 cucumber
ice cubes
1/4 lime
1 mint sprig
40ml (1 1/3oz) vanilla vodka

TO DECORATE

thin slices of pear
1 mint sprig

Cut the pear and cucumber into pieces. Place them in a liquidizer filled with ice cubes. Add the juice from the lime quarter, the mint sprig and the vanilla vodka. Blend and serve in a tall glass. Decorate with thin slices of pear arranged in a fan shape and held in place with a cocktail stick.

THE RULES OF A GOOD *cocktail*

There are numerous variations in the rules for making cocktails, and these can vary from one country to another. Here, we look at those in a French bar, which are the result of tried and tested know-how and proven tasting expertise. Even if sometimes, of course, you do not hesitate to break them!

1

USE ONLY ONE SPIRIT AS YOUR BASE

This rule might surprise you as it is common to enjoy cocktails made from a mix of several different spirits but it is far better to concentrate on a cocktail's star spirit and aim to enhance it. The French are well in tune with the art of tasting, which is so important to a wine-producing country.

2

DO NOT EXCEED 70ML (2⅓OZ) OF ALCOHOL PER COCKTAIL

The concept of 'consuming less but better' also lies at the heart of a bartender's concerns. The art of the cocktail is about the pleasure of enjoying a quality spirit in an elegant way while, at the same time, sharing a global experience as you appreciate its flavour. Today, cocktails that are lower in alcohol are available and promote their organoleptic qualities while also allowing for the possibility of a second glass.

3

THE 'THREE S' RULE

This is the gold standard for making a cocktail. Bartenders who are constantly searching for better, more balanced cocktails can rely on the 'three S' (3 Ss) rule to achieve this. It refers to the initial letters of the words 'sweet, sour and strong' (which, in the language of cocktail-making translates as 'softness', 'acidity' and 'strength'. Sweetness in a cocktail can come from fruit juice, a syrup, or even a fruit or plant cream liqueur; acidity from citrus fruit or an acidic solution; and strength, or body, from a spirit. By following this rule of threes, your cocktail will have structure and the greatest likelihood of being well balanced.

AVOID MIXING INCOMPATIBLE INGREDIENTS

This may seem obvious but certain ingredients do not go well together and quite simply can make a cocktail undrinkable. The most obvious examples of this are lemon juice and dairy products or fizzy drinks and dairy-based liqueurs. In the first instance, the diary product will curdle and, in the second, it will develop a solid and potentially dangerous texture when drunk. However, this rule can be deliberately flouted, for example in the preparation of clarified cocktails where sour milk actually acts as a natural filter.

MATCH THE GLASS TO THE STYLE OF COCKTAIL

Nothing is more inappropriate than serving soup on a flat plate, and the same applies in the cocktail world. Choosing the correct glass is essential for ensuring an optimal tasting experience and each family, and each type, of cocktails calls for a predetermined style of glass (*see* pages 54–55). However, it will always be necessary to adapt the dosage of a cocktail to the glass, even if it is a fancy, novelty glass.

FOLLOW THE ORDER IN WHICH THE COCKTAIL IS MADE

This rule is no longer really respected by experienced bartenders but it remains an important one for budding cocktail-making apprentices. Pouring the ingredients containing the least alcohol into your shaker or mixing glass first will prove less expensive if you were to make a mistake over either the quantity or relevant ingredient, making the final destination of your cocktail not a glass but the bar sink.

VODKA

CHOCOLATE MINT VODKA

Pour the vodka and the chocolate mint syrup into a bottle. Mix and then serve in frosted glasses.

MAKES 800ML (28OZ)

600ml (20oz) vodka
200ml (7oz) chocolate mint syrup
(see note)

You can buy chocolate mint syrup from large supermarkets or from www.moninshopping.com. Alternatively, replace it with a classic sugar cane syrup and add three squares of dark chocolate and 1 mint sprig to each bottle.

VODKA MARY

MAKES 600ML (20OZ)

600ml (20oz) vodka
1 bunch of cherry tomatoes, halved
4 celery sticks
4 drops of Tabasco®
4 dashes of Worcestershire sauce
4 tsp celery salt
ice cubes

Pour the vodka into a bottle and add the halved cherry tomatoes, celery sticks, Tabasco, Worcestershire sauce and celery salt. Mix and leave to macerate in the refrigerate for 1 week. Serve with ice cubes.

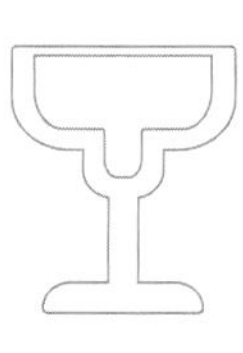

VODKA

JASMINE CRUSH

MAKES 1

5 or 6 mint leaves
1/4 orange, diced
10ml (2 tsp) cinnamon syrup
crushed ice
30ml (1 oz) cold jasmine tea
40ml (1 1/3 oz) lemon-flavoured vodka

TO DECORATE

1 thin slice of dried orange
1 cinnamon stick

Put the mint, diced orange and cinnamon syrup in an Old-Fashioned (whisky-style) glass and muddle the ingredients gently together. Half-fill the glass with crushed ice. Pour in the cold jasmine tea and the lemon-flavoured vodka. Mix well using a bar spoon. Decorate with a half slice of orange and a cinnamon stick.

VODKA

BLUE JEANS

MAKES 4

ice cubes
160ml (5¼oz) vodka
80ml (2⅔oz) blue Curaçao
80ml (2⅔oz) freshly squeezed lime juice
480ml (17oz) tonic water

Half-fill a cocktail shaker with ice cubes, pour in the vodka, blue Curaçao and lime juice, then shake. Strain into glasses and top up with the tonic water.

APPLE TROUBLE

MAKES 4

ice cubes
160ml (5¼oz) vodka
160ml (5¼oz) manzana verde (green apple) liqueur
60ml (2 oz) green apple syrup
420ml (15oz) soda water

Half-fill a cocktail shaker with ice cubes, pour in the vodka, green apple liqueur and green apple syrup, then shake. Strain into glasses and top up with the soda water.

RED PASSION

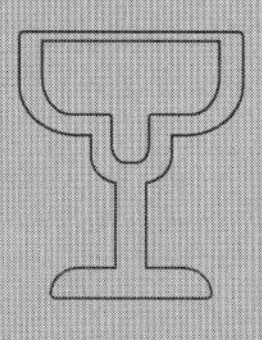

MAKES 1

ice cubes
40ml ($1\frac{1}{3}$oz) maracuja (passion fruit) juice
40ml ($1\frac{1}{3}$oz) strawberry juice
40ml ($1\frac{1}{3}$oz) cranberry juice
40ml ($1\frac{1}{3}$oz) orange-flavoured vodka

TO DECORATE

$\frac{1}{4}$ orange slice

Half-fill a cocktail shaker with ice cubes, pour in the maracuja juice, strawberry juice, cranberry juice and orange-flavoured vodka, then shake. Strain into the glass and decorate with a quarter orange slice.

VODKA MINOTAUR

MAKES 10

500ml (18oz) vodka
200ml (7oz) apricot liqueur
200ml (7oz) freshly squeezed lemon juice
100ml ($3\frac{1}{2}$oz) cinnamon syrup
2 apricots, cut into wedges
5 cinnamon sticks
500ml (18oz) ginger ale (Canada Dry®)
ice cubes
zest of 1 lemon

Pour all the liquid ingredients, except the ginger ale, into a large bowl. Add the fresh apricot wedges and cinnamon sticks. When ready to serve, top up with the ginger ale, add ice cubes and long thin strips of lemon zest.

VODKA

LEMONGRASS MOJITO

MAKES 1

10 mint leaves
½ lime, diced
10ml (2 tsp) lemongrass syrup
40ml (1⅓oz) vodka
crushed ice
50ml (1⅔oz) carbonated lemonade

TO DECORATE

1 mint sprig
1 stick of lemongrass

Put the mint leaves, lime and lemongrass syrup in a tumbler. Muddle the ingredients together and then add the vodka. Fill the glass with crushed ice and top up with the carbonated lemonade. Mix everything together, then decorate your mojito with mint sprig and a stick of lemongrass, cut into thin strips.

VODKA

RED BERRY MULE

MAKES 10

1 punnet of raspberries
1 punnet of blueberries
100ml (3½oz) sugar syrup
200ml (7oz) freshly squeezed lime juice
200ml (7oz) strawberry nectar (Alain Millat®)
400ml (14oz) vodka
75ml (2⅓oz plus 1 tsp) ginger beer

Put the raspberries in a liquidizer, add a little water and blend to a purée. Put a small blueberry in each cavity of an ice cube tray. Strain the raspberry purée and spoon it over the blueberries in the tray. Freeze for at least 3 hours. Pour the sugar syrup, lime juice, strawberry nectar and vodka into a bowl and stir. Chill in the refrigerator. Just before serving, finish by adding the ginger beer and the ice cubes.

VODKA

SPOTTED BEES

MAKES 10

400ml (14oz) vodka
200ml (7oz) passion fruit juice
100ml (3½oz) vanilla liqueur
100ml (3½oz) liquid honey
ice cubes
10 passion fruit
750ml (25oz) champagne *brut*

Pour all the liquid ingredients, except the champagne, into a large bowl. Stir with a bar spoon, then add ice cubes. Cut the passion fruit in half and scrape out the pulp into the bowl, reserving the shells of five. Mix again, then add the champagne. Stir lightly and serve with an empty half-shell of a passion fruit perched on top of each glass.

VODKA

MOSCOW COFFEE

MAKES 1

150ml (5oz) whipping or double cream
70ml (2⅓oz) hot black coffee
10ml (2 tsp) sugar cane syrup
50ml (1⅔oz) honey vodka

TO DECORATE

lime zest

Whip the cream until thick in a siphon, or in a bowl using a stand mixer or a hand-held mixer with a whisk attachment. Chill the cream in the refrigerator until ready to serve. Mix the coffee, sugar syrup and honey vodka together. Pour into a glass and top with a swirl of whipped cream. Decorate with a few strips of lime zest.

Old
Krupnik

VODKA

SOUR QUEEN

MAKES 10

500ml (18oz) vodka
400ml (14oz) freshly squeezed lemon juice
300ml (10oz) sugar syrup
10 dashes of Cherry Bitters
100ml ($3^1/_2$oz) port
plenty of ice cubes

TO DECORATE

amarena cherries

Pour all the liquid ingredients except the port into a liquidizer and blend. While the mixture subsides, add plenty of ice cubes to a large bowl. Then pour the liquid mixture into the bowl with the ice. Using a large spoon, carefully pour the port on top of the cocktail. Fill each glass with amarena cherries and pour the cocktail on top to serve.

LONG ISLAND ICED TEA

MAKES 10

100ml ($3^1/_2$oz) vodka
100ml ($3^1/_2$oz) gin
100ml ($3^1/_2$oz) white rum
100ml ($3^1/_2$oz) tequila
100ml ($3^1/_2$oz) Triple Sec
200ml (7oz) freshly squeezed lemon juice
1.5 litres (51oz) Coca-Cola®
ice cubes

Pour all the ingredients, except the Coca-Cola, into a large bowl. Add some ice cubes, then stir with a bar spoon. Add the Coca-Cola, which will sink to the bottom of the bowl, creating a layered effect.

VODKA TABERNACLE

MAKES 1

120ml (4oz) whipping or double cream
80ml (2⅔oz) vervain (lemon verbena) herbal tea
20ml (⅔oz) maple syrup
30ml (1oz) vodka
caramel sauce

Whip the cream until thick in a siphon, or in a bowl using a stand mixer or a hand-held mixer with a whisk attachment. Keep the cream chilled in the refrigerator until ready to serve. Prepare the infused verbena tea, pour it into a glass and add the maple syrup and vodka. Fill the glass with the whipped cream and carefully pipe or spoon the caramel sauce on top.

VODKA

TOMATO PASTEK

MAKES 1

30ml (1oz) green tea
$^1/_4$ watermelon
4 cherry tomatoes
2 basil sprigs
20ml ($^2/_3$oz) sugar cane syrup
40ml ($1^1/_3$oz) vodka
ice cubes

TO DECORATE

2 cherry tomato halves threaded onto a cocktail stick
small wedge of watermelon

Make the infused green tea and allow to cool. Dice the watermelon and cherry tomatoes and chop the basil sprigs. Blend all the ingredients in a liquidizer with some ice cubes. Pour into a fancy glass and serve with 2 cherry tomato halves threaded onto a cocktail stick and a small wedge of watermelon on the rim of the glass.

VODKA

RED UP

A little more complex to make but worth it for the pure pleasure of seeing and tasting it. Schweppes® agrum is a classic European mixer made from a combination of citrus fruits.

MAKES 1

FOR THE JELLY

10ml (2 tsp) spicy syrup (Monin®)
10ml (2 tsp) elderflower cordial
60ml (2 oz) cranberry juice
1 gelatine leaf

FOR THE COCKTAIL

1g (1 pinch) Espelette chilli powder
20ml (2⁄3oz) white grape juice
20ml (2⁄3oz) elderflower liqueur
20ml (2⁄3oz) sour rhubarb liqueur
40ml (1 1⁄3oz) vodka
60ml (2oz) Schweppes® agrum

Make a red jelly the day before: Pour the spicy syrup, elderflower cordial and cranberry juice into a small saucepan. Add the gelatine leaf and heat gently until dissolved. Set a glass at an angle, then pour the mixture into it and leave to set for 12 hours before standing the glass upright. The next day, prepare the cocktail by putting the Espelette red chilli powder, white grape juice, liqueurs and vodka in a cocktail shaker. Close the shaker and shake, then pour the mixture into the glass containing the red jelly. Finish with the Schweppes agrum.

MARS ATTACK

MAKES 1

FOR THE JELLY

10ml (2 tsp) green mint syrup
10ml (2 tsp) green mint liqueur
10ml (2 tsp) elderflower liqueur
60ml (2 oz) green tea
1 gelatine leaf

FOR THE COCKTAIL

20ml (2⁄3oz) pea juice (made from frozen peas mixed in a blender with a little water)
30ml (1oz) elderflower cordial
40ml (1 1⁄3oz) lemon-flavoured vodka
60ml (2oz) lemon Schweppes®

For the green jelly, prepare it in the same way as the red jelly above. The next day, prepare the liquid part of the cocktail by putting the pea juice, elderflower cordial and lemon-flavoured vodka in a cocktail shaker. Close the shaker and shake, then pour the mixture into the glass containing the green jelly. Finish with the lemon Schweppes.

3

TEQUILA & GIN

THE *cocktails*

TEQUILA & GIN

Whoever it was who said that white spirits have no taste must surely never have tried one of these subtly flavoured spirits, each one characterized by the singular way in which it is produced.

In the case of gin, juniper berries are macerated with other botanicals, such as coriander, lemon or angelica root, in a neutral alcohol produced from cereals. This manufacturing process delivers a rich aromatic intensity and gives the drinker a certain pleasure when tasting the pure spirit while also proving to be a key ingredient in the creation of a fine cocktail. The many different botanicals involved in the composition of gin mean that it blends perfectly with different types of ingredients and flavours, whether fruity, bitter or plant-based. Gin has experienced a resurgence in popularity in recent years and is particularly popular in the form of a Gin and Tonic.

Tequila, on the other hand, is uniquely distinctive because of the flavour derived from its raw material, blue agave. This is a common plant in Mexico where it grows in abundance, taking, on average, eight years to become sufficiently mature to be distilled into a spirit. Classic tequila cocktails have always been popular in the USA, due to the country's geographic proximity to Mexico. However, in Europe it has only recently been regarded as a high-quality spirit, most likely due to the fact that until the 1990s the only tequilas available were of poor quality and crucially contained no blue agave. Today, tequila is hugely popular in Europe, bringing success to many bars and delighting the taste buds of more and more drinkers tempted by this Mexican spirit.

TEQUILA & GIN MARGARITA

Both bitter-sweet and sweet-savoury, this cocktail was created in 1948 by Margarita Sames in Acapulco. It becomes a Grand Margarita when it is made with the French liqueur Grand Marnier Cordon Rouge, which is very popular in the USA.

MAKES 1

20ml (2/3oz) freshly squeezed lemon juice
30ml (1oz) triple sec Cointreau®
(or Grand Marnier Cordon Rouge
to make a Grand Margarita)
40ml (1 1/3oz) tequila
ice cubes

TO DECORATE

fine salt (*see* note)

Pour the lemon juice, triple sec (or Grand Marnier Cordon Rouge) and tequila into a cocktail shaker. Fill with ice cubes, close the shaker and shake energetically. Pour through a strainer into a cocktail glass.

Note

To frost just half the rim of the glass with salt, spread out a layer of fine salt in a saucer. Run half the edge of the glass against the zest of a lemon, then dip this part in the salt. Only half the rim of the glass is frosted to give the drinker the choice of enjoying the cocktail with or without salt.

TEQUILA & GIN

TEQUILA SUNRISE

Created in 1976 in San Francisco, this sunrise has been nominated the best cocktail in the world for its warm visual hues.

MAKES 1

ice cubes
80ml (2⅔oz) orange juice
40ml (1⅓oz) tequila
1 dash of grenadine syrup

Fill a glass with ice cubes and pour in the orange juice and tequila. Stir with a bar spoon and finish by adding the grenadine syrup. Stir gently to soften the colour.

GIN FIZZ

MAKES 1

ice cubes
15ml (½oz) sugar cane syrup (or 1 tsp icing sugar)
25ml (⅔oz plus 1 tsp) freshly squeezed lemon juice
40ml (1⅓oz) gin
soda water, to finish

Fill a cocktail shaker with ice and pour in the sugar cane syrup (or add the icing sugar), lemon juice and gin. Close the shaker and shake energetically. Strain into a tumbler without ice and top up with soda water.

TEQUILA & GIN

NEGRONI

SERVES 1

½ lemon slice
½ orange slice
ice cubes
40ml (1⅓oz) Campari
40ml (1⅓oz) gin

Put the lemon and orange half slices in a tumbler filled with ice cubes. Pour in the Campari and gin and mix.

GREEN FLOWER

MAKES 1

2 cucumber slices
6–8 coriander leaves
10ml (2 tsp) gomme syrup (or sugar cane syrup)
10ml (2 tsp) freshly squeezed lime juice
½ egg white
25ml (⅔oz plus 1 tsp) ginger liqueur (Ginger of the Indies®, Giffard®)
20ml (⅔oz) gin
ice cubes

TO DECORATE

1 coriander leaf

Muddle the cucumber and coriander leaves together in a cocktail shaker. Add the gomme syrup, lime juice, half egg white, the ginger liqueur and gin and fill the shaker with ice cubes. Close the shaker and shake energetically. Pour into a cocktail glass without ice, filtering out the ice cubes using a strainer. Serve decorated with a coriander leaf.

SCAR ONE

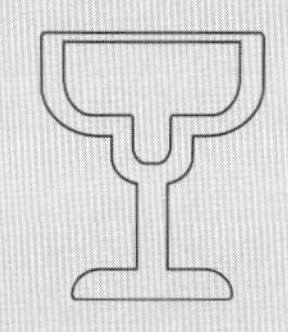

MAKES 1

6 large mint leaves
2 pineapple slices, diced
20ml (⅔oz) pineapple syrup
crushed ice
40ml (1⅓oz) tequila
passion fruit juice, to finish
pulp of ½ passion fruit

Muddle together the mint leaves and most of the diced pineapple (reserve a few dice for decoration) in a tumbler with the pineapple syrup. Fill the glass with crushed ice, add the tequila and finish by topping up with the passion fruit juice and the pulp of the passion fruit half. Stir with a bar spoon. Serve decorated with the reserved pineapple dice threaded onto a cocktail stick.

TEQUILA & GIN

SKY SPRITZ

MAKES 10

½ cucumber
150ml (5oz) elderflower syrup
150ml (5oz) freshly squeezed lemon juice
350ml (12oz) sweet-style gin (Plymouth® or Old Tom®)
350ml (12oz) fizzy water (Perrier® or similar)
ice cubes

TO DECORATE

10 thin strips of cucumber
thin wedges of grapefruit

Using a small melon baller, cut balls from the cucumber and place them in the cavities of an ice cube tray. Freeze for at least 3 hours. Mix all the ingredients, except the fizzy water and the ice cubes, together in a large bowl and keep chilled in the refrigerator. Immediately before serving, add the ice cubes and the fizzy water. Pour into glasses and decorate each with a strip of cucumber and a grapefruit slice.

POM POM

MAKES 1

¼ fennel bulb
½ pomelo, peeled
20ml (⅔oz) ginger syrup
½ egg white
40ml (1⅓oz) gin
ice cubes
tonic water, to finish (Schweppes®)

Cut the fennel bulb and peeled pomelo into pieces and blend in a liquidizer with the ginger syrup. Put the half egg white in a cocktail shaker (without ice), and shake. Add the mixture from the liquidizer and add to the shaker with the gin. Shake for about 10 seconds and strain into a glass with ice cubes. Top up carefully with the tonic water, without losing the foam.

TEQUILA & GIN PALOMA

MAKES 10

500ml (18oz) tequila
200ml (7oz) freshly squeezed lime juice
200ml (7oz) pink grapefruit juice
200ml (7oz) honey
750ml (25oz) prosecco
ice cubes
10 lime slices
10 strips of grapefruit zest

Pour all the ingredients except the prosecco and ice cubes into large bowl. Keep chilled in the refrigerator. Just before serving, add ice cubes and the prosecco. Stir lightly with a bar spoon. Decorate each glass with a lime slice and a curl of grapefruit zest.

TEQUILA & GIN

RED LION

Fill a cocktail shaker with ice cubes. Pour in the orange juice, lemon juice, Grand Marnier Gordon Rouge liqueur and gin. Close the shaker and shake energetically. Strain into a cocktail glass.

MAKES 1

ice cubes
15ml (½oz) freshly squeezed orange juice
15ml (½oz) freshly squeezed lemon juice
30ml (1oz) Grand Marnier Cordon Rouge® liqueur
30ml (1oz) gin

RED & YELLOW BIRD

MAKES 4

160ml (5¼oz) gin
480ml (17oz) freshly squeezed orange juice
160ml (5¼oz) Campari
4 half-slices lemon

Pour the gin, orange juice and Campari into a mixing glass and stir to mix. Pour into glasses and add a half-slice of lemon to each.

TEQUILA & GIN

SÃO LEOPOLDO

MAKES 1

40ml (1⅓oz) gin
20ml (⅔oz) elderflower liqueur
10ml (2 tsp) lime juice
ice cubes
40–60ml (1⅓oz–2oz) Guarana Antarctica®
strip of lime zest
1 slice of fresh ginger

Pour the gin, elderflower liqueur and lime juice into a wine tumbler. Fill the tumbler with ice cubes and finish with the Guarana Antarctica. Add the lime zest and slice of fresh ginger to the tumbler.

Note

Guarana Antarctica is a typical Brazilian fizzy soft drink made from guarana fruit, which can now be found outside of Brazil. Take care when drinking it as its caffeine content is quite high.

TEQUILA & GIN

PANCHO PARTY

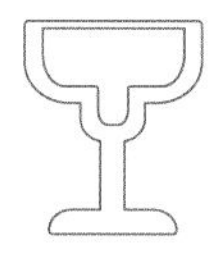

MAKES 1

3 strawberries
1 tbsp brown sugar
ice cubes
juice of 1/2 lime
40ml (1 1/3oz) tequila

Remove the hulls from the strawberries and cut them in half. Put them in a cocktail shaker, add the brown sugar and crush them together using a muddler. Add about 10 ice cubes, the lime juice and the tequila. Close the shaker and shake energetically, then pour the mixture through a strainer into a glass. Serve well chilled.

MAYA

MAKES 1

ice cubes
40ml (1 1/3oz) tequila
25ml (2/3oz plus 1 tsp) pear nectar
1 tbsp wildflower honey
black peppercorns

Fill a cocktail shaker with ice cubes and pour in the tequila, pear nectar and honey. Close the shaker and shake vigorously. Pour through a strainer into a glass. Finish by adding a grind of black pepper from a mill. Serve well chilled.

TEQUILA & GIN

SECOND CHANCE

MAKES 10

400ml (14oz) tequila
200ml (7oz) freshly squeezed lime juice
200ml (7oz) agave honey
400ml (14oz) fresh pineapple juice
1 rosemary sprig
200ml (7oz) ginger ale
ice cubes

TO DECORATE

pineapple leaves
rosemary sprigs

Pour all the liquid ingredients, except the ginger ale, into a large bowl and add a rosemary sprig. Just before serving, stir the mixture, then add the ginger ale and ice cubes. Decorate with pineapple leaves and rosemary sprigs.

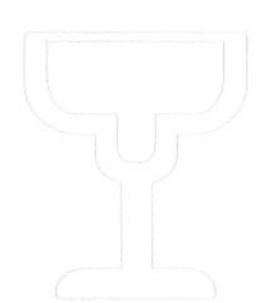

CANNON BALL

MAKES 4.5 LITRES (152OZ)

1.5 litres (51oz) tequila
1.35 litres (46oz) melon purée
900ml (30oz) freshly squeezed lime juice
450ml (16oz) agave honey
ice cubes
½ melon
1 tbsp poppy seeds

Pour all the liquid ingredients into a cocktail fountain or large bowl. Mix, then add some ice cubes. Using a melon baller, cut small balls from the melon half and dust them with the poppy seeds. Decorate the glasses with melon balls threaded onto wooden cocktail sticks.

TEQUILA & GIN

JAMAICAN FLOWER

MAKES 1

30g (1 oz) bissaps (dried hibiscus flowers)
20g (¾oz) icing sugar
40ml (1⅓oz) Katún® gin

Infuse 20g (⅔oz) of the bissaps in 1 litre (34oz) water at 80°C (176°F) for 3 hours, then strain. Next prepare a bissap syrup by putting the remaining 10g (⅓oz) bissaps in a saucepan with the icing sugar and 200ml (7oz) water. Warm over a low heat, stirring until the mixture becomes a syrup, then strain. Leave to cool. Pour the gin into a glass, add 250ml (9oz) of the infusion and 10ml (2 tsp) of the cold syrup.

Note

You can also use 1 sachet of bissap (hibiscus) infusion and ready-made syrup that can be bought in food stores.

TEQUILA & GIN

CHA CHA LOVE

For the white-pepper infused tequila: add 6g (1/8oz) white peppercorns to a 700ml (24oz) bottle of tequila and leave to infuse for 72 hours at room temperature. Strain before using to make your cocktails.

MAKES 1

40ml (1⅓oz) white pepper-infused tequila (*see* left)
20ml (⅔oz) red fruits liqueur (Chambord® liqueur or Mûroise® Giffard)
20ml (⅔oz) strawberry juice
20ml (⅔oz) raspberry juice
10ml (2 tsp) elderflower syrup
ice cubes

TO DECORATE

raspberries

Pour the white pepper infused tequila, red fruits liqueur, fruit juices and elderflower syrup into a cocktail shaker. Fill the shaker with ice cubes and shake energetically for 5–10 seconds. Strain directly into a wine glass filled with ice. Decorate with raspberries.

DRAGON FRUIT

MAKES 1

1 dragon fruit
40ml (1⅓oz) gin
30ml (1oz) freshly squeezed lime juice
120ml (4oz) freshly squeezed orange juice
10ml (2 tsp) sugar cane syrup
ice cubes

TO DECORATE

Lime zest (optional)

Slice off the top part of the dragon fruit and carefully scoop out the flesh with a spoon. Put the flesh in a liquidizer and blend. Strain the juice from the fruit through a conical sieve or strainer. Clean the liquidizer. Add all the ingredients to it, along with the ice cubes and blend for a about 10 seconds. Serve the cocktail in the hollowed out dragon fruit. Finally decorate with lime zest.

THE *cocktail* FAMILIES

'Cocktail families' refers to the generic names of recipes that use the same ingredients. These family names usually appear within a cocktail's title, helping the consumer to anticipate the drink's final taste. Here are names of some of the best-known families.

Punch

The term 'punch' derives from the Hindi word *panch*, meaning five. After 1632, it came to refer to a mixed drink, rather than a family of cocktails, and it was particularly popular with the British colonialists and the Royal Navy. The composition of a punch is therefore based on five ingredients: a Batavian arak spirit, an Indian black tea such as Darjeeling, a sweet base, lemon juice and spices. Make it ahead in the original style by adding the ingredients directly to a punch bowl and serving in cups.

Old-Fashioned

The first time the word 'cocktail' made its official appearance in the USA was on 13 May 1806 in a local newspaper in New York State. A similar style of drink had existed before the name cocktail was coined, which was a range of beverages called bitter slings made with a mixture of sprits, sugar and aromatic bitter concentrate. With the passage of time and changing fashions, these drinks eventually become known as 'old-fashioned' in homage to those first cocktails. They are made directly in an Old-Fashioned glass over ice.

SOUR

This cocktail family plays an important part in the world of mixing since the majority of cocktails are based on the 'Three S' rule (the rules of a good cocktail, *see* page 92). Here, by contrast, we find a base of spirits, lemon juice and sugar (in liquid or powdered form). Variations are possible by adding egg white to emulsify and enhance texture. Made in a shaker and served in a stemmed cocktail glass for a classic version or in an Old-Fashioned glass over ice for one made with egg white.

FIZZ

A first cousin to the sour family, it follows the basic structure of the sour, adding sparkling water to give the cocktail the 'fizzy' sensation that appeals so much to our taste buds. As with the sour, there are variations and these once again involve eggs. Adding an egg white gives you a Silver Fizz, while an egg yolk makes a Golden Fizz. Made in a shaker and served in a tall tumbler-type glass, without ice for the classic version and over ice for variations.

COLADA

Popularized in 1954 thanks to the famous Piña Colada, which originated at the Hilton Caribe hotel in San Juan, Puerto Rico, the colada family is based on spirits, milk, coconut cream or coconut water and fruit juice. Made in a cocktail shaker or liquidizer, it is served in a long class with ice cubes or crushed ice, whichever you prefer.

JULEP

Julep comes from the Arabic word *julâb*, meaning rose water. Originally it was the name given to sweetened medicinal drinks based on distilled water and orange blossom. In the early 1800s, a drink was introduced in the southern states of the USA called Mint Julep. It has many variations but this cocktail family owes its identity to the use of fresh mint as its main ingredients. It is made directly in a tumbler known as a mint julep cup, and served with crushed ice.

TEQUILA & GIN

TEQUILA BOOM

MAKES 6 SHOOTERS

120ml (4oz) tequila
120ml (4oz) tonic water (Schweppes®)
6 drops red chilli sauce

TO DECORATE

6 small red chillies

Pour 20ml (⅔oz) of tequila into each shooter glass and top up with the tonic water. Add a drop of red chilli sauce to each. Place a red chili in each glass as decoration, firmly strike the base of the glass on the table or bar and drink while still fizzing.

CRANBERRY SMASH

MAKES 4.5 LITRES (152OZ)

1.5 litres (51oz) gin
1.35 litres (46oz) cranberry juice
900ml (30oz) freshly squeezed lime juice
450ml (16oz) brown sugar syrup
ice cubes
1 lime
2 rosemary sprigs

Pour all the liquid ingredients into a cocktail fountain or large bowl. Mix, then add some ice cubes. Cut the lime into slices and add to the cocktail fountain or bowl with the rosemary sprigs.

TEQUILA & GIN

BRONX

MAKES 1

ice cubes
10ml (2 tsp) fresh orange juice
15ml (½oz) Italian vermouth
(Martini Rouge®, for example)
15ml (½oz) dry vermouth
(Martini Dry®, for example)
30ml (1oz) gin

Fill a cocktail shaker with ice cubes and pour in the orange juice, vermouths and gin. Close the shaker and shake energetically. Strain into a glass without the ice cubes.

Note

Vermouth is a wine-based aperitif, better known under the brand names of Martini, Cinzano and also Dry Noilly Prat (a French vermouth produced in Marseilles).

CENTRAL PARK
TENNIS COURTS
North Meadow
East Meadow
Jacqueline Kennedy Onassis Reservoir
METROPOLITAN MUSEUM OF ART
OBELISK
Great Lawn
DELACORTE THEATER
BELVEDERE CASTLE
The Ramble
BOAT HOUSE
BETHESDA FOUNTAIN & TERRACE
BANDSHELL
THE FRICK COLLECTION
ASIA SOCIETY MUSEUM
WHITNEY MUSEUM OF AMERICAN ART
JEWISH MUSEUM
MT. SINAI HOSPITAL
MUSEUM OF THE CITY OF NEW YORK
MUSEO DEL BARRIO
NEW YORK HOSPITAL CENTER
East Dr
West Dr
5th Av
Madison Av
Park Av
Lexington Av
3rd Av
2nd Av
E. 107th St
E. 103rd St
E. 102nd St
E. 101st St
E. 98th St
E. 73rd St
E. 72nd St
E. 71st St
E. 70th St
E. 69th St
E. 68th St
E. 67th St
E. 66th St

TEQUILA & GIN

AY CARAMBA!

Fill a cocktail shaker with ice cubes and add the spicy sauce, agave syrup, lemon juice and tequila. Close the shaker, shake vigorously, then strain into a glass. Serve well chilled.

MAKES 1

ice cubes
1 tsp spicy sauce (for example *piri piri*)
10ml (2 tsp) agave syrup
10ml (2 tsp) freshly squeezed lemon juice
40ml (1⅓oz) tequila

GUADA

MAKES 1

ice cubes
15ml (½oz) freshly squeezed lime juice
20ml (⅔oz) Pama® liqueur (pomegranate liqueur)
30ml (1oz) tequila
white peppercorns

Fill a cocktail shaker with ice cubes and pour in the lime juice, pomegranate liqueur and tequila. Close the shaker, shake energetically and strain into a glass. Finish with a grind of white pepper from a mill. Serve well chilled.

TEQUILA & GIN
MANGO FLOWER

MAKES 10

400ml (14oz) tequila
200ml (7oz) elderflower liqueur
400ml (14oz) mango juice
100ml (3½oz) freshly squeezed lime juice
75ml (2⅓oz plus 1 tsp) sparkling peach drink
ice cubes

TO DECORATE

mango slices
strips of lime zest

Pour all the liquid ingredients, except the sparkling peach drink, into a large bowl. Stir with a bar spoon, then add ice cubes and the sparkling peach drink. Serve each glass decorated with a mango slice and strips of lime zest.

TEQUILA & GIN

MEXICAN GARDEN

MAKES 4 SHOOTERS

1 small piece of red pepper
2 black peppercorns
40ml (1⅓oz) tequila
3 drops of Worcestershire sauce
15ml (½oz) freshly squeezed lemon juice
60ml (2oz) tomato juice
2 drops of Bitter-Truth® Celery Bitters
ice cubes

TO DECORATE

4 bird's-eye chillies
4 cherry tomatoes, halved

Muddle the red pepper with the black peppercorns in a cocktail shaker. Add the tequila, Worcestershire sauce, lemon juice, tomato juice and celery bitters. Fill the shaker with ice cubes, close it and shake energetically for 5–10 seconds. Filter twice, once through a strainer and then through a miniature conical sieve. Pour the mixture into the shooter glasses. Just before serving, decorate each drink with a bird's-eye chilli and 2 cherry tomato halves.

RED PEPPER SOUR

MAKES 1

20ml (⅔oz) freshly squeezed lemon juice
15ml (½oz) spiced syrup (Monin® Spicy)
15ml (½oz) red pepper juice (*see* Note)
40ml (1⅓oz) tequila
ice cubes

TO DECORATE

1 bird's-eye chilli (optional)

Pour the lemon juice, spiced syrup, red pepper juice and tequila into a cocktail shaker. Fill the shaker with ice cubes, close it and shake energetically. Strain into a Martini glass. Decorate with a bird's-eye chilli, if liked.

Note

You can make red pepper juice using either a juice extractor or a liquidizer. If using a liquidizer, remove the stalk and seeds from a red pepper and cut the flesh into dice. Place in the liquidizer, add a little mineral water (about 100ml/3½oz) and blend until smooth. Press through a conical strainer set over a bowl to collect the juice. Alternatively, put the pepper through a juice extractor, following the manufacturer's instructions.

TEQUILA & GIN

FRESH AIR

MAKES 10

400ml (14oz) gin
400ml (14oz) Martini® Bianco
200ml (7oz) freshly squeezed lemon juice (about 4 lemons)
100ml ($3\frac{1}{2}$oz) sugar syrup
1.5 litres (51oz) lemonade
lemon thyme sprigs
ice cubes

TO DECORATE

lemon thyme sprigs
1 orange

Add all the liquid ingredients, except the lemonade, to a large bowl and stir to mix. Add some lemon thyme sprigs, reserving some for decoration. Keep chilled in the refrigerator. When ready to serve, add ice cubes and the lemonade to the bowl.
Cut the orange into slices and then each slice in half. Serve in tall glasses, decorating each glass with the reserved lemon thyme sprigs and a half slice of orange.

TEQUILA & GIN

SPICY TEQUILA COFFEE

MAKES 4

200ml (7oz) whipping or double cream
2g chilli powder
200ml (7oz) sugar cane syrup
60ml (2oz) tequila
120ml (4oz) hot black coffee

TO DECORATE

4 bird's-eye chillies

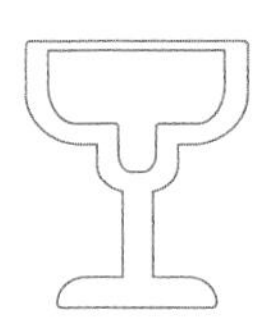

Mix the cream and chilli powder together, then whip in a siphon, or in a bowl using a stand mixer or a hand-held mixer with a whisk attachment, until just holding its shape. Keep chilled. Mix the sugar cane syrup and tequila together then heat. Divide between 4 tall heatproof glasses. Incline each cup and carefully pour hot coffee on top. Remove the piece of chilli from the whipped cream then spoon just enough on top of each drink to make three distinct layers. Decorate each glass with a small chilli and serve at once.

TEQUILA & GIN

DEATH PROOF

MAKES 4 SHOOTERS

4 cucumber slices
12–16 coriander leaves
20ml (⅔oz) gomme syrup (or sugar cane syrup, if unavailable)
200ml (7oz) freshly squeezed lime juice
1 egg white
50ml (1⅔oz) ginger liqueur (Ginger of the Indies, Giffard®)
ice cubes
40ml (1⅓oz) gin

Muddle the cucumber and coriander leaves together in a cocktail shaker. After that, add the gomme syrup, lime juice, egg white and the ginger liqueur. Fill the shaker with ice cubes, close it and shake energetically. Strain the mixture into 4 glasses. Just before serving, warm the gin in a small saucepan over a low flame and flambé. Pour the flaming gin into the glasses.

FIRE BOMB

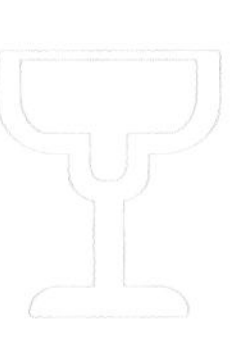

MAKES 6 SHOOTERS

120ml (4oz) tequila
30ml (1oz) sugar syrup
90ml (3oz) absinthe
6 sugar cube quarters soaked in absinthe

Divide the tequila and sugar syrup evenly between 6 shooter glasses. Heat the absinthe in a small saucepan (or a ladle with a spout) over a low flame and flambé. Pour the flaming absinthe into the glasses. Serve with the absinthe-soaked sugar cube quarters.

TEQUILA & GIN

LIMONCELLO CONCERTO

MAKES 10

500ml (18oz) limoncello
200ml (7oz) gin
200ml (7oz) freshly squeezed lemon juice
ice cubes
1.5 litres (51oz) citron soda
1 bunch of fresh mint

Pour all the ingredients, except the ice cubes, citron soda and the mint, into a large bowl. Stir and place in the freezer, if possible, or the refrigerator for 3 hours so the mixture is very cold. Just before serving, add ice cubes, the soda and mint. Stir with a bar spoon, then serve immediately in champagne coupes.

TEQUILA & GIN PARISIAN PUNCH

MAKES 4.5 LITRES (152OZ)

1.5 litres (51oz) gin
1.35 litres (46oz) elderflower cordial
900ml (30oz) freshly squeezed lemon juice
450ml (16oz) absinthe
ice cubes
1 cucumber

TO DECORATE

cucumber strips
edible flowers

Pour all the liquid ingredients into a cocktail fountain. Mix, then add some ice cubes. Cut the cucumber into thin slices and add them to the fountain. When serving, decorate each glass with a cucumber strip and an edible flower.

TEQUILA & GIN

GOLDEN TONIC

MAKES 10

250ml (9oz) freshly squeezed lemon juice
200ml (7oz) mineral water
edible gold leaf flakes
350ml (12oz) gin
700ml (24oz) tonic water

Pour the lemon juice into the cavities in an ice cube tray without filling them completely. Mix the mineral water with the edible gold leaf flakes and pour carefully into the cavities in the tray. Freeze for at least 3 hours. Pour the gin into a large bowl, add the tonic water and finally the ice cubes.

CHAMPAGNE

THE cocktails

Champagne is one of France's most celebrated wine AOCs (*Appellation d'Origine Contrôlée*), its reputation radiating out around the world thanks to its elegant bubbles, the result of generations of expertise.

The Champagne *terroir* abounds with vineyards on which three major grape varieties dominate: Pinot Noir, Pinot Meunier and Chardonnay. Once pressed, the grapes are put in barrels and following an initial fermentation are blended with non-sparkling wines from different harvests. This is the key stage for champagne to obtain its flavour. The wine is then bottled with yeasts and sugars which will enable it to transform itself into a sparkling wine. This second fermentation, which creates the mousse, is what sets it apart from the world's other sparkling wines, as only champagne will spend long months in the cellar working its magic. It will take about 15 months for champagne *brut* and 36 months for vintage champagne.

We may be familiar with champagne being simply poured into a flute or coupe, but it can also be used in many delicious cocktails. The fine bubbles will enhance the flavour of the other ingredients with which it is mixed and add freshness and lightness to the cocktail. Champagne will also create a slightly drier, more subtle drink, its luxurious reputation delivering prestige and elegance. In terms of other flavours, champagne complements powerful spirits like Cognac but also fresher ingredients such as fruits, which add a lovely flavour. In addition to mixing, champagne can also be served alongside a cocktail to refresh the drinker's palate between sips, allowing them to fully enjoy the cocktail's flavour.

CHAMPAGNE MOJITO ROYALE

A Cuban cocktail with a French twist. For a touch of luxury, champagne is added to the most popular classic cocktail in the world.

MAKES 1

3 mint sprigs
½ lime, diced
10ml (2 tsp) sugar cane syrup
1 tsp brown sugar
ice cubes or crushed ice
50ml (1⅔oz) Cuban rum
champagne *brut*, to finish

TO DECORATE

1 small mint sprig

Put the mint sprigs, diced lime, sugar cane syrup and brown sugar in a tumbler and crush together using a muddling tool. Fill the glass with ice cubes or crushed ice. Pour in the rum and then finish by topping up with champagne. Stir using a bar spoon and decorate with a small mint sprig. Serve with a stirrer and a straw.

CHAMPAGNE

CHAMPAGNE PUNCH

MAKES 10

150ml (5oz) freshly squeezed lime juice
150ml (5oz) sugar cane syrup
150ml (5oz) triple sec liqueur (Cointreau®, Grand Marnier®)
1 orange, thinly sliced
750ml (25oz) champagne *brut*

Add the lime juice, sugar cane syrup and liqueur to a large bowl and stir. If you have a liquidizer, blend the mixture for 10 seconds and then return it to the bowl. Add the orange slices and keep chilled in the refrigerator. Just before serving, finish by adding the champagne. Stir and serve in coupes.

CHAMPAGNE

MIMOSA

MAKES 1

10ml (2 tsp) Grand Marnier Cordon Rouge® liqueur
60ml (2oz) freshly squeezed orange juice
champagne *brut*, chilled, to finish

TO DECORATE

mimosa flower (optional)

Pour the Grand Marnier liqueur and orange juice into a champagne flute, then finish by topping up with chilled champagne. Stir with a bar spoon. Decorate with a mimosa flower, if liked.

Note

Take care to pour the champagne slowly into the glass as if you do it too quickly, the cocktail will froth up and overflow.

CHAMPAGNE

BELLINI

MAKES 10

350ml (12oz) peach nectar
100ml (3½oz) sugar cane syrup
ice cubes
750ml (25oz) champagne *brut*

Add the peach nectar and sugar cane syrup to a large jug. Add ice cubes to fill the jug. Stir and then add the champagne. Stir using a ladle and pour into champagne flutes to serve.

ROSSINI

MAKES 10

350ml (12oz) raspberry nectar
100ml (3½oz) sugar cane syrup
ice cubes
750ml (25oz) champagne *brut*

Add the raspberry nectar and sugar cane syrup to a large bowl. Add ice cubes to fill the bowl. Stir and then add the champagne. Stir using a ladle and spoon into champagne coupes to serve.

CHAMPAGNE

CHAMBORD COCKTAIL

MAKES 10

400ml (14oz) Chambord® liqueur
1.1 litres (37oz) champagne *brut*

Chill the Chambord liqueur and the champagne in the refrigerator. Just before serving, pour the liqueur into a large bowl and add the champagne. Stir and serve in flutes.

CHAMPAGNE

PINK ISLAND

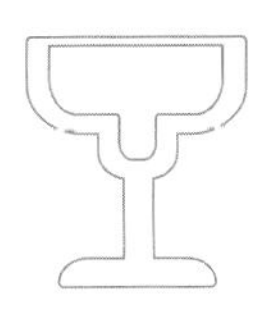

MAKES 10

500ml (18oz) strawberry nectar ice cubes
1 litre (34oz) rosé champagne

Pour the strawberry nectar into the cavities of an ice cube tray. Freeze for at least 3 hours. Put ice cubes into a large bowl and then pour in the champagne. Stir and serve in champagne coupes.

CHAMPAGNE

FLY TO THE MOON

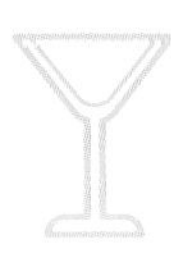

MAKES 10

100ml ($3^{1}/_{2}$oz) elderflower syrup
200ml (7oz) freshly squeezed lemon juice
200ml (7oz) blue Curaçao
200ml (7oz) raspberry vodka
750ml (25oz) champagne *brut*
ice cubes

Pour all the ingredients, except the champagne, into a large bowl filled with ice cubes. Stir with a bar spoon and keep chilled in the refrigerator. Just before serving, add the champagne and serve in champagne coupes.

CHAMPAGNE

FROM MONACO

To prepare the sweet mix, pour 200ml (7oz) cassis (blackcurrant) syrup and 30ml (1oz) blackberry purée into a bottle and shake vigorously. The mixture will keep for up to 3 days in the refrigerator.

MAKES 1

ice cubes
100ml (3½oz) champagne *brut*, well chilled
40ml (1⅓oz) sweet mix (*see* left)

TO DECORATE

1 redcurrant sprig

Fill a wine glass with ice cubes and pour in the well-chilled champagne. Carefully add the 40ml (1⅓oz) sweet mix, without combining the two. Decorate with a redcurrant sprig.

BLUE OCEAN

This blend of exotic flavours is the magical colour of tropical oceans...

MAKES 1

20ml (⅔oz) lychee juice
20ml (⅔oz) blue Curaçao
20ml (⅔oz) lychee liqueur (for example, Soho®)
ice cubes
champagne *brut*, to finish

TO DECORATE

1 lychee

Pour the lychee juice, blue Curaçao and lychee liqueur into a cocktail shaker filled with ice cubes. Close the shaker and shake vigorously for 5–10 seconds. Strain the mixture into a flute. Rinse the shaker with a little champagne and strain this into the flute. Finish by topping up with champagne and decorate with a lychee, opened out to look like a flower.

CHAMPAGNE

FROM GENEVA

MAKES 1

20ml (2/3oz) strawberry syrup
20ml (2/3oz) peach purée
20ml (2/3oz) red fruits liqueur
ice cubes
champagne *brut*, to finish

TO DECORATE

1/4 strawberry
peach slice

Put the strawberry syrup, peach purée and red fruits liqueur into a cocktail shaker. Fill the shaker with ice cubes, close it and shake energetically for 5–10 seconds. Strain the mixture into a champagne flute. Rinse the shaker with a little champagne, pour it into the flute and finish by topping up with chilled champagne. Decorate with a strawberry quarter and a thin peach slice.

BARBOTAGE

MAKES 1

10ml (2 tsp) grenadine
20ml (2/3oz) freshly squeezed lemon juice
40ml (1 1/3oz) freshly squeezed orange juice
ice cubes
champagne *brut*, to finish

Put the grenadine, lemon juice and orange juice in a cocktail shaker. Fill the shaker with ice cubes, close it and shake energetically. Strain the mixture into a champagne flute and finish by slowly topping up with champagne. Stir gently with a bar spoon.

cocktails IN FILM & TELEVISION

Cocktails certainly did not wait for the arrival of cinema to become popular with drinkers – a gap of almost ninety years separates them – but it is undeniable that some of these stylish drinks have clearly benefitted from being in the spotlight again or, quite simply, made themselves better known to a much wider audience.

Casino Royale

If we can credit Jeremiah P. Thomas with being the father of the Dry Martini cocktail, there is no question that it was the novelist Ian Fleming who really put it on the map, turning it into a huge hit with consumers with the publication of his book *Casino Royale* in 1953. In the film adaptation of the book, released in 2006, Britain's most famous spy, James Bond, can be seen at a poker table in a casino in Montenegro opposite his antagonist and enemy, Le Chiffre. James Bond calls the barmen over and says:
'A dry martini,
'Oui, monsieur.
'Wait...three measures of Gordon's, one of vodka and half a measure of Kina Lillet. Shake it over ice and then add a thin slice of lemon peel.
'Yes, sir.'

And so the famous Vesper Martini was born in honour of the beautiful Vesper Lynd, because 'once you've tasted it, that's all you want to drink'.

VESPER MARTINI

MAKES 1

90ml (3oz) Gordon's® London dry gin
30ml (1oz) vodka
15ml (½oz) Lillet® Blanc
ice cubes

TO DECORATE

thin slice of lemon zest

Pour the ingredients into a cocktail shaker filled with ice. Shake and serve in a martini glass without ice. Decorate with a thin slice of lemon zest.

Kina Lillet, as specified when Bond orders the drink, is no longer produced and has since been replaced with Lillet Blanc.

Cocktail

If one film in this section not only raised the profile of cocktails but also proved the inspiration for a whole generation of future bartenders, then it was the 1988 film, *Cocktail*, starring Tom Cruise in the standout role of Brian Flanagan. Throughout the film, the audience watches a dazzling array of cocktails being made, each more legendary than the last – Martini, Cuba Libre, Piña Colada, Old-Fashioned and even a Blue Lagoon – with nothing left on the table. They also marvel at the acrobatics of *flair bartending*, a totally original and previously unseen way of cocktail shaking, which remained very popular until the early 2000s. Red Eye, the film's star cocktail created by Douglas Coughlin, is reputedly the best cure for a hangover.

RED EYE

MAKES 1

180ml (6oz) lager-style beer
90ml (3oz) tomato juice
1 whole egg, with an unbroken yolk
2 aspirins (extremely optional and not recommended)

Mix all the ingredients in a 500ml (18oz) beer glass without adding ice. Drink it down in one and you are ready to go again, just like Douglas Coughlin in the film.

The Big Lebowski

When the film opened in American cinemas in 1998, Jeff Lebowski, aka The Dude, unwittingly found himself dubbed 'the first hipster'. His singular style of long hair, goatee beard and oversize clothes, totally at odds with the fashions of the day, no doubt played their part but, above all, it was his love of a White Russian that made a lasting impression and turned the film into a classic. This celebrated cocktail, which he cannot live without, became an icon for the audience. As a result cocktail bars were inundated with orders for it made 'the Dude way' (a somewhat abstract challenge for bartenders as Jeff would switch from milk to cream, or even milk powder during the course of the film). A variation of the Black Russian, both cocktails owe their name to the addition of vodka in the recipe.

WHITE RUSSIAN

MAKES 1

50ml (1⅔oz) Russian vodka
20ml (⅔oz) Kahlúa® coffee liqueur
30ml (1oz) milk or pouring cream
ice cubes

Pour the ingredients into an Old-Fashioned glass. Fill with ice cubes, stir and enjoy straight away.

Miami Vice

In this 2006 film adaptation of the famous 1984 American TV show featuring two Miami undercover detectives, James 'Sonny' Crockett reveals his penchant for Mojitos. As someone who lived on a sailboat with an alligator called Elvis and owned an offshore catamaran and luxury racing car, this should come as no surprise. When Sonny asks Isabella for a drink, she asks what he would like and he replies, 'I'm a friend of Mojitos.' Isabella's immediate response is: 'I know a place', and seconds later they are aboard a speedboat, where she tells him they're going to enjoy their Mojitos in Havana at La Bodeguita Del Medio, the historic bar where Ernest Hemingway used to drink his.

MOJITO

MAKES 1

2 tsp icing sugar
juice of ½ lime
2 mint sprigs
90ml (3oz) soda water
45ml (1½oz) Havana Club® 3 year old rum
ice cubes

Put the sugar, lime juice and mint in a tumbler. Pour in the soda water and muddle the ingredients together very gently (the object is to mix rather than crush them). Add the rum, then fill the glass with ice cubes. Give the mojito a final stir using a straw.

Sex And The City

Carry Bradshaw and her girlfriends influenced an entire generation from the end of 1990s until the early 2000s. In this series, four like-minded pals showed us, among other things, the joys of discovering fashion and love. In episode 19 of season 2, Samantha is heard ordering a Cosmopolitan at a wedding reception. Despite the cocktail having been created in 1988 by Toby Cecchini at The Odeon restaurant in New York (and even though Madonna was seen with one at a Grammy's party in the early 1990s), it was not until the show's screenwriters showcased it in this way that its popularity went viral among consumers. Given time, this fashion phenomenon will settle down and the 'Cosmo' will become a modern classic cocktail.

COSMOPOLITAN

MAKES 1

45ml (1½oz) Absolut® lemon vodka
22ml (¾oz) Cointreau® triple sec
22ml (¾oz) cranberry juice
22ml (¾oz) freshly squeezed lime juice
ice cubes

TO DECORATE

¼ lime

Pour all the ingredients into a cocktail shaker. Fill three-quarters with ice cubes. Shake for 10 seconds, then strain into a Martini-style cocktail glass without ice. Decorate with a lime quarter.

Mad Men

Set in the New York of the mid-1960s, this series was first broadcast in July 2007 and developed a cult following. It follows the life of Don Draper, the charismatic creative director of the city's Sterling Cooper agency, and during the course of the episodes we are introduced to all of Don's vices, including alcohol. Each of the main cocktail families makes an appearance, allowing us to discover, in turn, the Manhattan, Whiskey Sour and Mint Julep. However, bourbon and rye whiskey did not monopolize the screen time because during the 1960s Russian vodka producers, such as Stolichnaya and Smirnoff, broke onto the US market, and so we see Don enjoying a Dry Vodka Martini, a Bloody Mary or a White Russian. Gin also earns its place in a Gimlet, while rum enhances a Mai Taï, Blue Hawaii or Piña Colada. However, *the* star cocktail of the series remains the Whiskey Old-Fashioned (made with bourbon or rye), thanks to a never-to-be-forgotten scene where Don, with impeccable style, climbs over the bar to mix the drink himself, admittedly in a rather hit-and-miss way for purists, but with flair nonetheless.

WHISKEY OLD-FASHIONED

MAKES 1

1 white sugar cube
3 dashes of aromatic bitters
a splash of soda water
60ml (2oz) bourbon or rye whiskey
ice cubes

TO DECORATE

orange zest
1 maraschino cherry

Infuse the sugar cube with the aromatic bitters, place it in an Old-Fashioned glass and add the soda water. Crush the sugar cube to dissolve it, then pour in half the whiskey. Add some ice cubes, stir to mix, then add the rest of the whiskey with some more ice cubes. Stir and serve decorated with orange zest and a maraschino cherry.

CHAMPAGNE CITY LIGHTS

MAKES 10

200ml (7oz) sugar syrup
350ml (12oz) freshly squeezed lemon juice
350ml (12oz) strawberry liqueur
350ml (12oz) pisco
750ml (25oz) champagne *brut*
ice cubes
orange slices
blackberries

TO DECORATE

orange zest twists

Pour all the ingredients, except the champagne, into a large jug or bowl. Fill with ice cubes, add the orange slices and blackberries and keep chilled. Just before serving, add the champagne and then pour into champagne flutes decorated with orange twists.

CHAMPAGNE

OXYGEN

The champagne bubbles will bring you extra pizzaz in this glamorous confection.

MAKES 1

20ml (2/3oz) raspberry syrup
20ml (2/3oz) lychee liqueur
20ml (2/3oz) passion fruit juice
ice cubes
champagne *brut*, well chilled, to finish

TO DECORATE

1 lychee
1 raspberry

Pour the raspberry syrup, lychee liqueur and passion fruit juice into a cocktail shaker. Fill the shaker with ice cubes, close it and shake energetically for 5–10 seconds. Strain the mixture into a champagne flute. Rinse the shaker with a little champagne and pour this into the flute, then top up with well-chilled champagne. Decorate with the peel of a lychee cut in the shape of a flower with a raspberry placed in the centre.

THE TEMPLE

Cognac and champagne are two of French soil's most incomparable *terroirs*!

MAKES 1

20ml (2/3oz) passion fruit juice (or pulp of 1/2 passion fruit)
20ml (2/3oz) cranberry juice
20ml (2/3oz) cognac
ice cubes
champagne *brut*, well chilled, to finish

TO DECORATE

1 small bunch of redcurrants

Put the passion fruit juice (or pulp), cranberry juice and cognac in a cocktail shaker. Fill the shaker with ice cubes, close it and shake energetically for 5–10 seconds. Strain the mixture into a champagne coupe. Rinse the shaker with a little champagne and pour this into the coupe, then top up with well-chilled champagne. Decorate with a small bunch of redcurrants.

CHAMPAGNE SGROPPINO

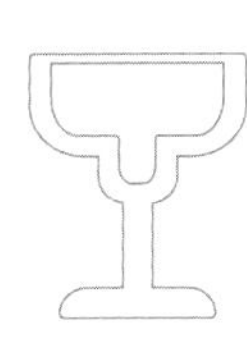

MAKES 10

100ml (3½oz) limoncello, well chilled
10 scoops of lemon sorbet
750ml (25oz) champagne *brut*

TO DECORATE

10 strips of lemon zest

Pour the well-chilled limoncello into a large bowl, add the lemon sorbet and, using a whisk, mix until combined and the mixture liquifies. Add the champagne and serve in champagne flutes. Decorate with a strip of lemon zest tucked into top of each glass.

CHAMPAGNE

FRENCH 75

MAKES 10

200ml (7oz) sugar syrup
400ml (14oz) freshly squeezed lemon juice
500ml (18oz) Plymouth® or Old Tom® gin
750ml (25oz) champagne *brut*
ice cubes

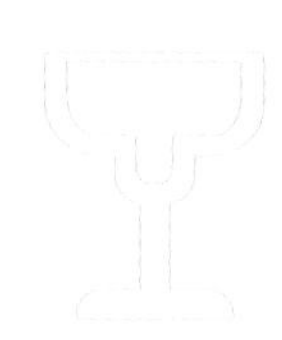

TO DECORATE

1 lime, thinly sliced

Pour all the ingredients, except the champagne, into a large bowl. Fill with ice cubes. Stir with a bar spoon and keep chilled. Just before serving, add the champagne and lime slices to the bowl. Serve in champagne coupes.

CHAMPAGNE

CHAMPAGNE COCKTAIL

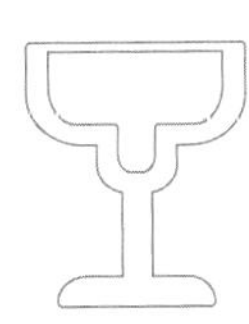

MAKES 10

100ml ($3^1/_2$oz) sugar syrup
100ml ($3^1/_2$oz) cognac
10 dashes of Angostura® bitters
750ml (25oz) champagne *brut*
ice cubes

TO DECORATE

dried orange slices

Pour all the ingredients, except the champagne, into a large bowl. Stir with a bar spoon, then keep chilled. Just before serving, add the champagne and dried orange slices.

CHAMPAGNE

PARIS CHIC

MAKES 10

4g (1/8oz) agar agar
300ml (10oz) pink grapefruit juice
200ml (7oz) lychee juice
ice cubes
750ml (25oz) champagne *brut*
200ml (7oz) elderflower liqueur
100ml (3 1/2oz) soda water

Mix the agar agar with the pink grapefruit juice and lychee juice in a saucepan. Bring the mixture to the boil and then pour into a large heatproof bowl. When the mixture has cooled, place the bowl in the refrigerator overnight so the mixture sets into a jelly. Just before serving, add ice cubes to the bowl, then pour in the champagne, elderflower liqueur and soda water. Stir with a bar spoon and serve. Provide spoons for your guests so they can help themselves to some of the jelly.

CHAMPAGNE PINK FLOYD

MAKES 10

100ml (3½oz) vodka
200ml (7oz) strawberry liqueur
400ml (14oz) lychee juice
200ml (7oz) pink grapefruit juice
750ml (25oz) champagne
100ml (3½oz) rose syrup
ice cubes

TO DECORATE

20 amarena cherries

Pour all the liquid ingredients, except the champagne and the syrup, into a large bowl. Add ice cubes and stir. Add the champagne and last of all the syrup to create a two-layer effect. Serve in champagne flutes decorated with two amarena cherries on a cocktail stick.

CHAMPAGNE

GASCON-STYLE CHAMPAGNE PUNCH

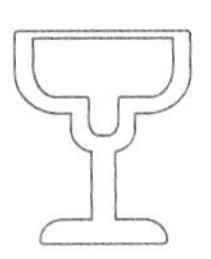

Pour the lemon juice, Floc de Gascogne and Armagnac into a large bowl. Fill with ice cubes. Stir with a bar spoon until chilled. Just before serving, finish by adding the champagne.

MAKES 10

150ml (5oz) freshly squeezed lemon juice
150ml (5oz) white Floc de Gascogne
100ml (3½oz) Armagnac
ice cubes
750ml (25oz) champagne

FRANCHE-COMTÉ-STYLE CHAMPAGNE PUNCH

MAKES 10

150ml (5oz) freshly squeezed lemon juice
50ml (1⅔oz) liquid honey
100ml (3½oz) Pontarlier absinthe
ice cubes
750ml (25oz) champagne

Pour the lemon juice, honey and absinthe into a large bowl. Fill with ice cubes. Stir with a bar spoon until chilled. Just before serving, finish by adding the champagne.

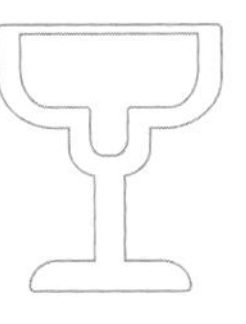

CHAMPAGNE PICK ME UP

MAKES 10

100ml ($3\frac{1}{2}$oz) grenadine syrup
300ml (10oz) freshly squeezed orange juice
400ml (14oz) cognac
750ml (25oz) champagne
ice cubes

Pour all the ingredients, except the champagne, into a large bowl. Fill with ice cubes. Stir with a bar spoon and keep chilled. Just before serving, add the champagne. Serve in champagne coupes.

CHAMPAGNE

AMERICAN FLYER

MAKES 10

100ml (3½oz) sugar syrup
100ml (3½oz) freshly squeezed lime juice
200ml (7oz) amber rum
750ml (25oz) champagne *brut*
ice cubes

Pour all the ingredients, except the champagne, into a large bowl. Fill the bowl with ice cubes. Stir with a bar spoon and keep chilled. Just before serving, add the champagne. Serve in champagne coupes.

CHAMPAGNE

AIR MAIL

MAKES 10

100ml (3½oz) liquid honey
200ml (7oz) freshly squeezed lemon juice
400ml (14oz) amber rum (Havana Club Especial®)
750ml (25oz) champagne *brut*
ice cubes

Pour all the ingredients, except the champagne, into a large bowl. Fill with ice cubes. Stir with a bar spoon and keep chilled. Just before serving, add the champagne. Serve in champagne coupes.

CHAMPAGNE

CHARENTES-STYLE CHAMPAGNE PUNCH

MAKES 10

150ml (5oz) freshly squeezed lemon juice
150ml (5oz) Pineau des Charentes
100ml ($3\frac{1}{2}$oz) cognac
ice cubes
750ml (25oz) champagne

TO DECORATE

thin dried orange slices

Pour the lemon juice, Pineau des Charentes and cognac into a large bowl. Fill with ice cubes. Stir with a bar spoon until chilled. When ready to serve, finish by adding the champagne and decorate with thin slices of dried orange.

5

WHISKY & COGNAC

THE *cocktails*

WHISKY & COGNAC

'What a waste to dilute a spirit that has matured for so long in a cask!' is what you are likely to hear from a friend who has never had the chance to taste a good Bourbon Old-Fashioned or a Manhattan. What a mistake that would be on their part!

Even the emergence of the term cocktail, coined in 1806 by a journalist from *The Balance, and Columbian Repository*, referred to a spirit drink served during a campaign evening in the state of New York, consisting of whisky, sugar and an aromatic bitter. This mix also gave its name to the bittered sling group of cocktails, which would later become the Old-Fashioned family.

Whiskies and cognacs aged for many years in oak barrels are imbued with a very rich aromatic palette, due mainly to their contact with the wood during maturation.

Whisky will bring spicy, woody and even sour notes to a cocktail, while cognac adds woody notes and notes of honeyed crystallized fruits. This aromatic richness is particularly interesting as it allows you to create cocktails using very few ingredients or, conversely, to increase the number of ingredients without altering the spirit's very powerful flavour.

WHISKY & COGNAC

IRISH COFFEE

MAKES 1

15ml (½oz) sugar cane syrup
40ml (1⅓oz) Irish whiskey
40ml (1⅓oz) hot black coffee
30ml (1oz) whipping cream, whipped

Heat the sugar cane syrup and Irish whiskey together and pour this hot mixture into a heatproof glass with a handle. Tilt the glass and carefully pour the coffee down the side of the glass so as to keep the layers of whiskey and coffee clearly separate. Stand the glass upright again and, using a bar spoon, very gently spoon a layer of whipped cream on top of the coffee to create three distinctly separate layers.

WHISKY & COGNAC

MY MEDICINE

MAKES 10

400ml (14oz) bourbon
200ml (7oz) apple juice
100ml (3½oz) freshly squeezed lemon juice
100ml (3½oz) sugar syrup
10 sage leaves
750ml (25oz) dry cider
ice cubes

Pour all the ingredients, except the dry cider and ice cubes, into a large bowl. Mix, then chill in the refrigerator for a short while to let the sage leaves infuse. Just before serving, add the dry cider and ice cubes.

WHISKY & COGNAC

JACKY BLOT

MAKES 1

30g (1oz) thinly sliced pineapple
10ml (2tsp) gomme syrup (or sugar cane syrup)
ice cubes
60ml (2oz) 'sour mash' whiskey (Jack Daniel's®)
1 dash of orange bitters

TO DECORATE

orange zest
1 pineapple leaf

Place the pineapple slices in an Old-Fashioned glass, without crushing them, and add the gomme syrup. Fill the glass with ice cubes and pour in the whiskey. Finish with a dash of orange bitters. Serve decorated with strips of orange zest and a pineapple leaf.

WHISKY & COGNAC

TWIST & MINT

MAKES 1

150ml (5oz) green tea infused with juniper berries
40ml ($1^1/_3$oz) bourbon
100ml ($3^1/_2$oz) freshly squeezed grapefruit juice
20ml ($^2/_3$oz) agave syrup infused with essential lemon oil (*see* Note)
1 tablespoon peppermint flower water (available from organic stores or online)
ice cubes

Infuse the green tea and leave it to cool. Put all the ingredients into a cocktail shaker. Fill with ice cubes, close the shaker and shake for about 15 seconds. Pour into an attractive glass.

Note

To make the agave syrup infused with lemon, put two drops of essential lemon oil in a bottle of agave syrup. Shake and store until using (up to 1 year).

WHISKY & COGNAC

SIDECAR

Pour the lemon juice, triple sec and cognac into a cocktail shaker. Fill the shaker with ice, close it and shake energetically. Strain the cocktail before pouring into a Martini glass.

MAKES 1

10ml (2 tsp) freshly squeezed lemon juice
20ml (2/3oz) triple sec (Cointreau®)
40ml (1 1/3oz) cognac
ice cubes

THE GODFATHER

MAKES 1

ice cubes
30ml (1oz) amaretto liqueur
40ml (1 1/3oz) Scotch whisky

Fill an Old-Fashioned glass with ice cubes, pour in the amaretto liqueur, followed by the Scotch whisky. Stir using a bar spoon.

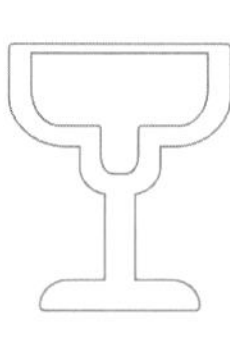

WHAT TO EAT WITH *cocktails*

WASABI PEAS

Preparation: 5 minutes
Cooking: 20 minutes

Preheat the oven to 100°C (220°F), Gas Mark ¼. Line a baking tray with baking parchment. In a bowl, mix 3 tablespoons wasabi with 250g (9oz) peas and some salt, then rub between your hands to distribute the wasabi evenly. Spread out the peas on the baking tray and bake for 20 minutes, turning them over regularly. Switch off the oven, leaving the peas inside to cool.

FLAKY POPPY SEED TWISTS

Preparation: 5 minutes
Cooking: 10 minutes

Preheat the oven to 180°C (350°F), Gas Mark 4. Line a baking sheet with baking parchment. Cut a ready-rolled sheet of puff pastry into 20 strips. Beat 1 egg yolk with a little water to dilute it and brush over the pastry strips. Sprinkle with 1 tablespoon poppy seeds. Turn the strips over and repeat. Twist each strip, lay them on the baking sheet, then bake for 10 minutes. Sesame seeds or dried herbs can be substituted for the poppy seeds.

Cocktails often mean aperitifs, and of course aperitifs mean nibbles! Now that you have become a pro with a cocktail shaker, it's time to have a go at making some small bites to serve with your favourite drinks. Whether for everyday or more special occasions, it's time to discover recipes that will transform you into the aperitif and cocktail king or queen!

COURGETTE FRIES

Preparation: 10 minutes
Cooking: 15 minutes

Preheat the oven to 200°C (400°C), Gas Mark 6. Line a baking sheet with baking parchment and have ready 3 bowls. Cut 2 small courgettes into thin sticks, place them in the first bowl and mix with 10 tablespoons plain flour and 2 tablespoons herbes de Provence. Beat 2 eggs in the second bowl. Mix 70g (2½oz) breadcrumbs with 10 tablespoons grated Parmesan in the third bowl. Coat the courgette sticks first in the egg, then breadcrumbs, then spread them out on the baking sheet and bake for 10–15 minutes.

SPICY YOGURT DIP

Preparation: 5 minutes

Empty 1 small tub of Greek yogurt into a liquidizer. Add ½ garlic clove, ¼ tomato, diced, ½ small red pepper, deseeded and diced, and a few coriander sprigs. Blend until smooth and creamy. Keep refrigerated. Serve with raw vegetable dippers.

CRAB, AVOCADO & EXOTIC FRUIT SALAD

Preparation: 10 minutes
Resting: 30 minutes

Drain 1 can of white crab meat and flake it into a bowl with a fork. Mix in the finely grated zest and juice of ½ lime, a few chopped blades of chives, 1 finely chopped shallot and 1 pinch each of salt and red chilli flakes. Peel 2 kiwi fruits, cut a slice from a mango and chop both fruits into small cubes. Add them to the crab and stir to mix. Leave to rest in the refrigerator for 30 minutes.

PRAWN TEMPURA

Preparation: 15 minutes
Resting: 30 minutes
Cooking: 5 minutes

Whisk together 100g (3½oz) plain flour, 50g (1¾oz) cornflour, 1 teaspoon baking powder, 1 teaspoon curry powder, 1 egg yolk, 150ml (5oz) cold water, salt and pepper until you have a smooth batter. Leave to rest in the refrigerator for 30 minutes. Peel 16 large prawns, leaving on the tail part. Heat oil for deep-frying to between 160–180°C (325–350°F). Coat the prawns in the batter and deep-fry in the hot oil for 5 minutes until golden. Drain on kitchen paper and serve the prawns with a spicy spring roll dipping sauce.

PAIN D'ÉPICES TOASTS WITH PÂTÉ

Preparation: 10 minutes
Resting: 30 minutes

Lightly toast 3 slices of *pain d'épices* (a soft-textured French loaf flavoured with honey and sweet spices). Cut each slice into quarters and spread a little fig jam on top. Cut 2 slices of pâté into 12 cubes and place one on each square of toast. Season with salt and pepper and sprinkle lightly with crushed pink peppercorns. Leave to rest in the refrigerator for 30 minutes.

SALMON TARTARE

Preparation: 10 minutes
Marinating: 30 minutes

Finely chop 200g (7oz) skinned salmon fillet and place in a serving bowl. Add 1 minced shallot, the finely grated zest and juice of 1 lime, 1 tablespoon olive oil, 2 teaspoons soy sauce, some pink peppercorns and 2–3 coriander sprigs, finely chopped. Season with salt and pepper and leave to marinate in the refrigerator for 30 minutes. Serve in small glasses.

WHISKY & COGNAC

SANTA'S LITTLE HELPER PUNCH

MAKES 4.5 LITRES (152OZ)

1.5 litres (51oz) rye whiskey
900ml (30oz) red vermouth
135ml (4½oz) sweet cider
450ml (16oz) sugar syrup
10 dashes of Angostura® bitters
10 cinnamon sticks
8 whole cloves
ice cubes
1 orange
1 lemon

Pour all the liquid ingredients into a cocktail fountain or a large bowl and add the cinnamon sticks and cloves. Mix, then add some ice cubes. Slice the orange and lemon and add them to the cocktail fountain (or bowl). Mix again.

WHISKY & COGNAC

FRENCH MOJITO

MAKES 1

3 mint sprigs
½ lime, diced
10ml (2 tsp) sugar cane syrup
1 teaspoon brown sugar
ice cubes or crushed ice
50ml (1⅔oz) cognac
soda water, to finish

TO DECORATE

leaves from 1 mint sprig

Crush the mint sprigs, diced lime, sugar cane syrup and brown sugar together in a tumbler using a muddling tool. Fill the glass with ice cubes or crushed ice. Pour in the cognac and finish by topping up with soda water. Stir with a bar spoon. Decorate with the mint leaves.

DOCK OF THE BAY

Bay leaves are not just for cooking. They make a nice surprise in a cocktail.

MAKES 1

4 bay leaves
10ml (2 tsp) gomme syrup (or sugar cane syrup)
20ml (⅔oz) Scotch whisky liqueur
50ml (1⅔oz) bourbon whiskey
ice cubes (for the shaker and to serve)

TO DECORATE

2 bay leaves

Put the bay leaves, gomme syrup, Scotch whisky liqueur and bourbon whiskey in a cocktail shaker. Fill the shaker with ice cubes, close it and shake vigorously. Strain twice, once through a strainer and then through a miniature conical strainer. Serve in an Old-Fashioned glass filled with ice cubes and decorate with two bay leaves.

WHISKY & COGNAC

COGNAC IN CHINA

Cognac, France's traditional brandy, is very popular in China. This cocktail is dedicated to that country.

MAKES 1

2 strawberries
4 raspberries
4 blueberries
10ml (2 tsp) agave syrup
10ml (2 tsp) freshly squeezed lemon juice
1 small rosemary sprig
40ml (1⅓oz) cognac
ice cubes (for the shaker and to serve)
ginger beer (*see* Note), to finish

TO DECORATE

1 rosemary sprig
1 strawberry, sliced
1 raspberry
2 blueberries

Using a muddling tool, gently crush the strawberries, raspberries and blueberries in a cocktail shaker with the agave syrup and lemon juice. Add the rosemary and cognac. Fill the shaker with ice cubes, close it and shake vigorously. Strain twice, once through a strainer and then through a miniature conical sieve. Pour into a tall glass containing ice cubes and top up with ginger beer. Decorate with the sliced strawberry, a raspberry and two blueberries.

Look for ginger beer under the name of Fever Tree®.

DECORATING *cocktails*

Cocktail decorations have evolved with the times. Any decoration was originally part of the recipe and things such as a cherry soaked in brandy or a strip of citrus zest were added as a final touch to complement the cocktail's flavour. The arrival of Tiki bar culture brought with it small Chinese umbrellas and an entire plantation of fresh fruit as decorations. In the 1980s cocktails struggled to evolve and the infamous half slices of citrus fruit became ubiquitous. The late 1990s and the early 2000s marked a revival in the inclusion of fresh produce in mixes, which led to bartenders honing their skills for cutting fruits in precise ways. This led to the cocktail becoming not just good to drink but aesthetically pleasing, like the gastronomic dishes served in restaurants. Bartenders made a point of embellishing their cocktails while

still respecting some commonsense rules, such as only using produce that could be eaten or that related directly to the cocktail's ingredients.

From 2010 onwards, international bartenders began to develop a certain flair for style alongside their talents for creating flavours and their showmanship. Glassware became more diverse and everyday objects hijacked to become part of the cocktail. The scene was set for the customer to live the full cocktail bar experience.

Today, the trend is a return to minimalism and zero waste. Any leftovers from fruit used in recipes are dehydrated and used for decoration, citrus zests are reappearing and bartenders are championing the belief that 'less is more'. And lastly, a cocktail's decoration is mainly confined to carefully selected glassware in tune with the times.

WHISKY & COGNAC

STARFISH

MAKES 1

1 small melon, such as cantaloupe or ogen
100ml (3½oz) apple juice
1g (1 pinch) of green curry powder
40ml (1⅓oz) VSOP cognac
ice cubes
soda water, to finish

Cut the melon in half and remove the flesh using a spoon, discarding the seeds. Blend the flesh with the apple juice and curry powder. Trim the bottom of the melon shell so it stands upright. Pour the blended mixture into the melon and add the cognac. Serve immediately with ice cubes, topped up with soda water to finish, or chill and add the soda water just before serving with a straw.

Note

If you have a juice extractor, pass the melon flesh, 1 quartered apple and the curry powder through the machine. Pour the juice extracted into the melon shell, add the cognac and the ice. Stir.

SCOTCH & BERRIES

MAKES 1

3 strawberries
4 raspberries
1 teaspoon brown sugar
40ml (1⅓oz) Scotch whisky
30ml (1oz) cranberry juice
ice cubes
orange zest

Dice the strawberries and raspberries and place them in a cocktail shaker. Add the brown sugar and crush together using a muddling tool. Add the whisky, cranberry juice and ice cubes. Close the shaker and shake for about 10 seconds, then strain into a cocktail glass. Gently press a piece of orange zest between your fingers above the glass to release the essences.

WHISKY & COGNAC

OX BLOOD PUNCH

MAKES 4.5 LITRES (152OZ)

1.5 litres (51oz) bourbon
900ml (30oz) beetroot juice
900ml (30oz) freshly squeezed lemon juice
900ml (30oz) sugar syrup
2 tarragon sprigs
ice cubes

TO DECORATE

50g (1¾oz) unsalted beetroot crisps

Pour all the liquid ingredients into a cocktail fountain or a large bowl. Mix, then add the tarragon and some ice cubes. Serve in glasses decorated with unsalted beetroot crisps.

WHISKY & COGNAC

APRICOT JULEP

The freshness of mint, the sweetness of apricot and the power of cognac... It's time to have fun with this variation of a classic Mint Julep.

MAKES 1

8–10 mint leaves
20ml (⅔oz) *Abricot du Roussillon* liqueur (apricot liqueur)
crushed ice
30ml (1oz) cognac
finely grated zest of 1 lime

TO DECORATE

1 mint sprig
lime zest

Place the mint leaves and apricot liqueur in an Old-Fashioned glass and crush them together using a muddling tool. Fill the glass with crushed ice and pour in the cognac. Stir to mix using a bar spoon and add the lime zest for a citrussy 'zing'. To decorate, tuck a mint sprig in the crushed ice and add a thin twist of lime zest.

DIPSIE NUTSY

Dipsie knows how to surprise with its display of explosive flavours.

MAKES 1

40ml (1⅓oz) cognac
5ml (1 tsp) hazelnut syrup
5ml (1 tsp) white chocolate syrup
10ml (2 tsp) vanilla liqueur
10ml (2 tsp) spiced syrup (Spicy de Monin®)
20ml (⅔oz) egg white
1 generous teaspoon chestnut jam
ice cubes

TO DECORATE

1 vanilla pod

Place the cognac, hazelnut syrup, white chocolate syrup, vanilla liqueur, spiced syrup, egg white and chestnut jam in a cocktail shaker. Fill the shaker with ice cubes, close it, then shake vigorously. Strain into a Martini glass without ice. Serve decorated with a vanilla pod.

WHISKY & COGNAC

BIRD OF PARADISE

MAKES 1

60ml (2oz) hibiscus infusion (*see* page 141)
10ml (2 tsp) agave syrup
30ml (1oz) cognac
100ml (3½oz) milk
orange zest

Make the hibiscus infusion. Pour the agave syrup, hibiscus infusion and cognac into a heatproof glass. Foam the milk until mousse-like using a milk frother and spoon it on top of the hibiscus and cognac mix. Squeeze a strip of orange zest above the glass to release the essences.

WHISKY & COGNAC

ALEXANDER

MAKES 1

10ml (2 tsp) coffee-flavoured pouring cream
30ml (1oz) brown crème de cacao
40ml ($1\frac{1}{3}$oz) cognac
ice cubes

Pour the cream, crème de cacao and cognac into a cocktail shaker. Fill the shaker with ice cubes, close it, then shake energetically. Strain into a double martini glass.

It is worth knowing that a martini glass usually has a capacity of 70ml ($2\frac{1}{3}$oz), while a double martini glass holds between 120–150ml (4–5oz).

WHISKY & COGNAC

SHOW ME THE MONKEY

MAKES 1

ice cubes or crushed ice
100ml (3½oz) apple juice
25ml (⅔oz plus 1 tsp) Scotch whisky liqueur (Drambuie®)
50ml (1⅔oz) Monkey Shoulder® Scotch whisky

TO DECORATE

1 small mint sprig
1 slice of banana (optional)

Fill a cocktail shaker with ice cubes and pour in the apple juice, Drambuie liqueur and Monkey Shoulder Scotch whisky. Close the shaker and shake energetically. Strain into a tall tumbler filled with ice cubes or crushed ice. Decorate with a small mint sprig and a banana slice for the monkey!

MONKEY
SHOULDER

WHISKY & COGNAC

COGNAC SUMMIT

MAKES 1

4 slices of fresh ginger
ice cubes
1 strip of cucumber peel (optional)
40ml (1⅓oz) cognac
60ml (2oz) artisan lemonade
lime zest

Crush the ginger slices in an Old-Fashioned glass using a muddling tool. Fill the glass with ice cubes and, if you wish, add a strip of cucumber peel. Pour in the cognac and finish with the artisan lemonade. Stir with a bar spoon and add the lime zest to the glass.

FRENCH CAÏPIRINHA

MAKES 1

3 slices of fresh ginger
¼ lime
ice cubes
60ml (2oz) cognac
30ml (1oz) Guarana Antarctica®

TO DECORATE

1 long thin strip of cucumber

Place the ginger slices and lime quarter in a glass and crush using a muddling tool. Fill the glass with ice cubes, then pour in the cognac followed by the Guarana Antarctica. Add a long thin slice of cucumber threaded onto a wooden satay stick.

TRUE OR FALSE?

With long-established habits and differing ideas, our knowledge of spirits can sometimes be wrong. Do you want to test yours?

THE SYMBOL '40% VOL.' SHOWN ON A BOTTLE INDICATES THE LEVEL OF SUGAR CONTAINED IN A BARREL

FALSE. This symbol is the percentage of pure alcohol in the bottle. In this instance it would contain 40% pure alcohol and 59.9% water.

TO STORE A BOTTLE OF ALCOHOL CORRECTLY, IT MUST BE PROTECTED FROM LIGHT

TRUE. Bottles of alcohol do not like light as it can make their colour deteriorate over time. It is better to store your bottles in a dry, cool place, such as a cellar, away from light. Certain bottles, like vermouths, ports or wine-based aperitifs must be kept in the refrigerator after opening.

I WILL GET LESS DRUNK IF I DRINK A COCKTAIL THAT DOES NOT CONTAIN SUGAR

FALSE. Sugar does not increase the quantity of alcohol but it can mask it, making the cocktail somewhat easier to drink. Even if the quantity of pure alcohol in the blood does not change, a sweet cocktail can be drunk more quickly, which can increase the number of glasses and therefore the quantity of alcohol consumed.

WITH A GOOD CARDIO WORKOUT THE NEXT DAY, I WILL GET RID OF THE ALCOHOL I CONSUMED THE NIGHT BEFORE MORE QUICKLY

FALSE. Regardless of the length or difficulty of a workout, you can only eliminate 10% of alcohol from the body through the pores of the skin. The balance has to pass through your liver, so look after it.

DRINKING ALCOHOL AT WEEKENDS ONLY IS WORSE THAN DRINKING ALL WEEK

TRUE. Even if the study has not been proven, it would seem that drinking an excess of alcohol at weekends would be more harmful than drinking in moderation all week. In any event, it is worth having extended periods of abstinence and remain moderate in your consumption of alcohol at parties.

MEN TOLERATE ALCOHOL BETTER THAN WOMEN

FALSE. It is all about how heavy the drinker is. But it should be noted that women feel the effects of alcohol more rapidly due to their metabolism.

THE DARKER IT IS, THE BETTER THE SPIRIT

FALSE. Spirits have not managed to escape the widespread current practice of standardization. In the past, a rich mahogany colour indicated that it had been aged in a barrel for at least several years but spirits today, while still aged in barrels, are also enhanced with a caramel-type food colouring (E150a). This standardizes each year's production and allows consumers to find the same shade that first attracted them.

DRINKING COFFEE LOWERS ALCOHOL LEVELS

FALSE. Time is the only way to lower the level of alcohol in the blood. There is no miracle cure.

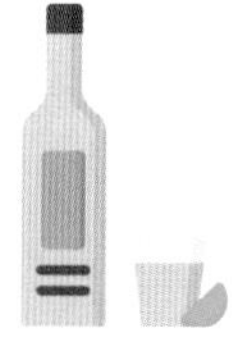

A VODKA COCKTAIL IS NO STRONGER THAN A GLASS OF WINE OR A BEER

TRUE. They each have an equal number of units. A cocktail made with 30ml (1oz) vodka at 40% will have the same amount of alcohol as a 100ml (3½oz) glass of wine at 12% or a 250ml (9oz) beer.

ALCOHOL WARMS YOU UP

FALSE. The sensation of heat is due to dilation of the blood vessels under the skin, but the warm glow feeling is simply an impression. Heat is only diverted from inside the body to surface areas. We believe we are hot but in fact our body temperature drops by 0.5°C (33°F) for every 50ml (1⅔oz) of alcohol we absorb. An excess of alcohol can therefore result in hypothermia.

YOU MUST STAY FULLY HYDRATED TO AVOID A HANGOVER

TRUE. But beware, drinking water will not lower your alcohol levels. The absorption of alcohol makes your body become very dehydrated. Drinking a glass of alcohol alternately with a glass of water allows you initially to better regulate your alcohol consumption and, importantly, to counteract this dehydration.

IT'S A RIP-OFF WHEN THE BAR TENDER PUTS LOTS OF ICE CUBES IN MY COCKTAIL

FALSE. This is a common belief but in fact the opposite is true since less is more in the bar world. Less ice means more dilution, which creates an imbalance in the cocktail due to its watery nature. A second rule is that cold seeks out cold. The more ice cubes added to a cocktail, the more slowly they will melt, neutralizing the wateriness. A cocktail will always be made with the standard measure of alcohol. Whether it is filled with ice or not, the measure remains the same. However, if only a little ice is added, the dilution will be greater and by the time you finish, your cocktail will be less well balanced.

I SHOULD KEEP TO THE SAME SPIRIT ALL EVENING TO AVOID A HANGOVER

FALSE. You can drink wine followed by whisky or vodka. The problem is not changing spirits but the quantity consumed. To avoid feeling ill the next day, it is better to drink in moderation, choosing high-quality spirits and wines.

WHISKY & COGNAC

JUST A COGNAC

Discover the alluring transparency of this summer cocktail, made to simply enjoy on a terrace or in the garden...

MAKES 1

ice cubes
20ml (2/3oz) fig syrup
50ml (1 2/3oz) cognac
40ml (1 1/3oz) artisan lemonade
2 dashes of peach bitters
4 white grapes

Fill a tasting glass with ice cubes and pour in the fig syrup and cognac. Stir with a bar spoon. Top up with the lemonade and add the peach bitters. Halve the grapes and add to the glass.

WHISKY & COGNAC

SCOTCH SOUR

Place the lemon juice, icing sugar and Scotch whisky in a cocktail shaker. Fill the shaker with ice cubes, close it and shake energetically. Strain into a martini glass. Decorate with a cherry infused with eau-de-vie.

MAKES 1

20ml (2/3oz) freshly squeezed lemon juice
1 teaspoon icing sugar
40ml (1 1/3oz) Scotch whisky
ice cubes

TO DECORATE

1 cherry infused with eau-de-vie

To qualify as Scotch, the whisky must be made in Scotland and matured in casks for a minimum of three years, preferably oak.

BERGAMOT FRUIT

MAKES 1

1 or 2 teaspoons of Earl Grey tea leaves
15ml (1/2oz) apricot liqueur
40ml (1 1/3oz) cognac
ice cubes

TO DECORATE

orange zest
1 basil leaf

Steep the tea in 100ml (3 1/2oz) boiling water for 3–4 minutes and then leave it to cool. Pour 50ml (1 1/3oz) of the strained cold tea into a cocktail shaker with the apricot liqueur and cognac. Fill the shaker with ice cubes, close it and shake energetically. Strain into a martini glass. Decorate with orange zest and a basil leaf.

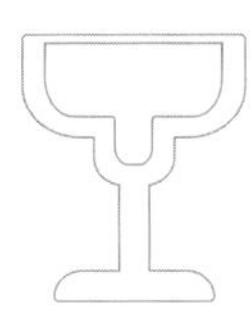

WHISKY & COGNAC
HOT CHOCOLATE

MAKES 1

50ml ($1^2/_3$oz) vanilla soya milk
120g ($4^1/_4$oz) milk chocolate, chopped
20ml ($^2/_3$oz) Mozart® White Chocolate liqueur
100ml ($3^1/_2$oz) chocolate syrup
50ml ($1^2/_3$oz) cognac

Pour the soya milk into a whipping siphon and fit it with two gas cartridges. Turn the siphon up and down so the gas can circulate. Chill the siphon in the refrigerator for 24 hours. Heat the chocolate in a saucepan over gentle heat until it melts. Add the liqueur, chocolate syrup and cognac and stir until evenly mixed. Pour into a heatproof glass and swirl soya milk mousse on top.

WHISKY & COGNAC

PINK PARADISE

MAKES 4

160ml (5¼oz) chamomile infusion
ice cubes
160ml (5¼oz) Rémy Martin® White cognac
80ml (2⅔oz) candy floss syrup
400ml (14oz) pink lemonade

Make up the chamomile infusion with boiling water and leave it to cool. Half fill a cocktail shaker with ice cubes, pour in the white cognac and candy floss syrup, close it and shake. Pour into glasses through a strainer and top up with pink lemonade.

CLEM

MAKES 4

ice cubes
120ml (4oz) freshly squeezed lemon juice
420ml (15 oz) clementine juice
80ml (2⅔oz) sugar cane syrup
180ml (6oz) whisky

Half-fill a cocktail shaker with ice cubes, pour in the lemon juice, clementine juice, sugar cane syrup and whisky and shake. Pour into glasses through a strainer.

WHISKY & COGNAC

AGNES'S TEMPTATION

MAKES 1

3 cherry tomatoes, halved
10ml (2 tsp) spiced winter berry cordial (or use blackcurrant cordial)
30ml (1oz) cranberry juice
30ml (1oz) bourbon
20ml (⅔oz) sour rhubarb liqueur

TO DECORATE

1 cherry tomato, halved
1 blackberry, halved

Place the cherry tomato halves in a cocktail shaker and add the winter berry cordial, cranberry juice, bourbon and sour rhubarb liqueur. Close the shaker, shake brisky, then pour directly without straining into an Old-Fashioned glass. Decorate with a cocktail stick threaded with the halved cherry tomato and blackberry.

Note

Spiced Winter Berries Cordial® has a more subtle flavour than traditional syrup and is similar to a concentrated juice, with the natural flavours of fruit and spices.

TAKE FIVE

MAKES 1

½ lime, cut into quarters
15ml (½oz) caramel syrup
30ml (1oz) apple juice
15ml (½oz) Mandarin Imperial Napoleon® liqueur
40ml (1⅓oz) cognac
ginger ale, to finish

Place the lime quarters in a tumbler, add the caramel syrup and crush together using a muddling tool. Pour the apple juice, mandarin liqueur and cognac into a cocktail shaker, shake well, and pour into the tumbler. Finish by topping up with ginger ale.

Note

For an even more indulgent cocktail, replace the caramel syrup with homemade runny caramel.

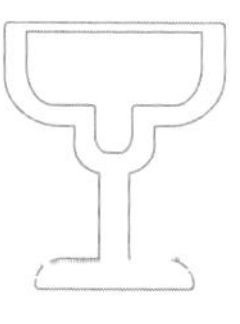

WHISKY & COGNAC

CHIWAWA

MAKES 1 SHOOTER

50ml ($1^2/_3$oz) spirit (whisky, rum or another of your choice)
½ sugar cube

Pour the spirit of your choice into a shot glass. Set the alcohol alight using a cigarette lighter or blowtorch. Place the sugar cube in a spoon or on a fork and hold it over the glass a few centimetres away from the flame. Leave the sugar to melt and fall gently as caramel to the bottom of the glass. Extinguish the flame and drink the cocktail, taking care not to burn yourself!

WHISKY & COGNAC

PERFUME NO.1

MAKES 1

50g (1/3 cup) diced cucumber
10ml (2 tsp) elderflower syrup
10ml (2 tsp) freshly squeezed lemon juice
20ml (2/3oz) L'Esprit de June vine flowers liqueur
50ml (1 2/3oz) cognac
ice cubes

Crush the diced cucumber with the elderflower syrup and lemon juice in a cocktail shaker using a muddling tool. Add the vine flowers liqueur and cognac. Fill the shaker with ice cubes, close it and shake energetically. Strain twice, once through a strainer and then though a mini-conical sieve. Serve without ice.

Note

Straining the cocktail twice enables you to catch the ice cubes in the strainer and then the cucumber pulp when you use the fine-mesh miniature conical sieve.

WHISKY & COGNAC

MANHATTAN

MAKES 10

15 cherries infused with eau de vie
30 drops of Angostura® bitters
350ml (12oz) red vermouth (Martini®, Cinzano®)
700ml (24oz) rye whiskey or bourbon

Place the cherries in the cavities of an ice cube tray and add a little water and 2 drops of Angostura bitters to each. Freeze for at least 3 hours. Tip the cherry ice cubes directly into a large bowl, then pour in the red vermouth and rye whiskey. Stir and serve in Old-Fashioned glasses.

OTHER SPIRITS

THE *cocktails*

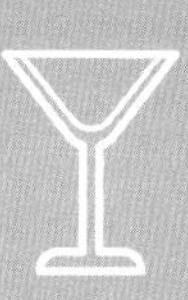

OTHER SPIRITS

The popularity of cocktails today is the result both of the talents of bartenders and the wide range of spirits produced around the world offering such a choice of different flavours. The expertise of master distillers and cellar masters also provides a growing opportunity to develop new recipes, each one more surprising than the last.

When we talk about drinks made with spirits, however, we must not forget aperitifs, which bartenders have considered with renewed interest for a number of years now. After all, aperitifs offer the chance to suggest cocktails with a lower alcohol content, allowing the customer to take greater advantage of the diversity of the cocktail menu.

This is why vermouths, bitters and even aniseed-flavoured drinks are back in the spotlight. As a result, Aperol® has enjoyed huge success thanks to the Spritz cocktail that mixes it with prosecco, sparkling water and orange. In the same way, Suze, long regarded as a spirit 'of the past' is becoming increasingly trendy. Artisan and ancestral liqueurs are not being left behind either; their addition to a cocktail brings fullness, power and aromas that deliver delight when tasted.

Setting out to discover both French and international spirits is always interesting due to the wide choice on offer. Their impact on your cocktails will be instant, bringing subtlety or character, depending on the desired aromatic profile. Indulge in a tasting session and have fun with the different products available. As is the case with cooking, you need to give something a try, and sometimes get it wrong, in order to create a true masterpiece!

OTHER SPIRITS

STROMBOLI

MAKES 1

10ml (2 tsp) grenadine syrup
ice cubes
30ml (1oz) grappa
50ml (1⅔oz) dry Italian white wine

Pour the grenadine syrup into a shaker. Fill with ice cubes and add the grappa and white wine. Close the shaker and shake, then strain into a champagne coupe glass.

GRASSHOPPER

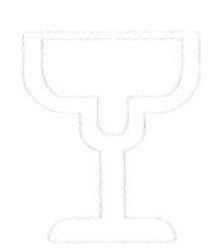

MAKES 10

40g (1½oz) agar agar
500ml (18oz) white chocolate liqueur
700ml (24oz) Get 27®
ice cubes
500ml (18oz) pouring cream

Mix the agar agar with the white chocolate liqueur (cold) in a saucepan. Bring the mixture to the boil, then pour it into a large bowl. Leave to cool before putting the bowl in the refrigerator overnight so the jelly can set. Pour the Get 27 into the bowl, add some ice cubes, then drizzle over the cream. Just before serving, stir the Get 27 and cream into the mixture. Have spoons available for your guests to come and serve themselves with jelly.

OTHER SPIRITS

CHILE PUNCH

MAKES 4.5 LITRES (152OZ)

1.5 litres (51oz) pisco
900ml (30oz) apricot liqueur
1.35 litres (46oz) freshly squeezed lemon juice
450ml (16oz) peach syrup
ice cubes
1 lemon
10 peach halves

Pour all the liquid ingredients into a cocktail fountain. Mix, then add some ice cubes. Cut the lemon into slices and add to the cocktail fountain with the peach halves. Mix again.

OTHER SPIRITS

CHAMOMILE & ME

MAKES 1

3 saffron threads
1 drop of ylang-ylang flower water
1 tsp acacia honey
120ml (4oz) chamomile tea
30ml (1oz) lime eau de vie (Mette®)

Place the saffron threads and ylang-ylang flower water in a jar of acacia honey. Leave for about 1 week, making sure to stir the honey once a day. Make up the chamomile tea, add 1 teaspoon of the honey and pour in the lime eau de vie. Stir and drink hot.

B-52

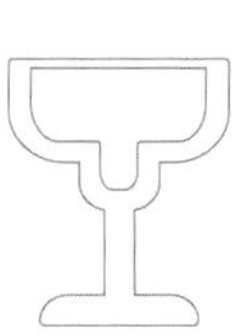

MAKES 1 SHOOTER

20ml (⅔oz) coffee liqueur
20ml (⅔oz) whiskey cream liqueur (Bailey's®)
20ml (⅔oz) Grand Marnier Cordon Rouge® liqueur

Pour the coffee liqueur into a heatproof shooter glass. Position a teaspoon horizontally in the glass against the inner wall and very carefully pour the whiskey cream over the back of it to create a separate layer. Clean the spoon and then gently pour in the Grand Marnier Cordon Rouge liqueur in the same way. The Grand Marnier can first be heated in the microwave or in a pan to make easier to flambé. Set light to the cocktail.

OTHER SPIRITS

GREEN BEAST

MAKES 10

2 cucumbers, plus extra for decoration
350ml (12oz) lime juice cordial
350ml (12oz) Pernod® absinthe
700ml (24oz) still mineral water

TO DECORATE

cucumber slices
cucumber balls

Cut the cucumbers into small pieces and blend them to a juice in a liquidizer. Strain the juice and pour it into the cavities of an ice cube tray. Freeze for at least 3 hours. Add the cucumber ice cubes to a large bowl and pour in the lime juice cordial, absinthe and mineral water. Stir and serve, decorating each glass with cucumber slices and a cucumber ball.

OTHER SPIRITS

SUMMER CUCUMBER

MAKES 1

2 cucumber slices
2 strawberries
1 sage leaf
ice cubes
20ml (2⁄3oz) Menthe Pastille® liqueur (Giffard)
10ml (2 tsp) grapefruit syrup
30ml (1oz) tonic water (Schweppes®)

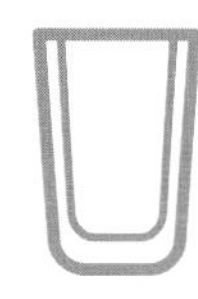

TO DECORATE

2 cucumber slices
1⁄4 strawberry

Crush the cucumber slices, strawberries and sage leaf in a cocktail shaker using a muddling tool. Fill the shaker with ice cubes, then add the Menthe Pastille and grapefruit syrup. Close the shaker and shake vigorously. Strain into a tumbler filled with ice cubes. Finish with the tonic water and add the cucumber slices and strawberry quarter to the glass as decoration.

OTHER SPIRITS

GARDEN PARTY COCKTAIL

MAKES 4.5 LITRES (152OZ)

2 litres (68oz) green chartreuse
1.35 litres (46oz) freshly squeezed lime juice
900ml (30oz) sugar syrup
soda water
ice cubes
1 lime

Pour the chartreuse, lime juice and sugar syrup into a cocktail fountain or a large bowl and finish with the soda water. Mix, then add some ice cubes. Slice the lime, add the slices to the cocktail fountain or bowl and mix again.

FEE BROTHERS
1864
INT BITTER
(PEPPERMINT)
For Flavoring Purposes
4 FL OZ (118 ml)

OTHER SPIRITS

AMARETTO SOUR

MAKES 1

10ml (2 tsp) sugar cane syrup
20ml (2/3oz) freshly squeezed lemon juice
1 egg white
40ml (1 1/3oz) Amaretto liqueur

TO DECORATE

1 cherry infused with eau de vie

Add the sugar cane syrup, lemon juice, egg white and Amaretto liqueur to a cocktail shaker. Close the shaker, shake and pour through a strainer into a cocktail glass. Decorate with a cherry infused with eau de vie.

OTHER SPIRITS

SPARKLING NORMAN PUNCH

MAKES 10

150ml (5oz) freshly squeezed lemon juice
150ml (5oz) sugar syrup
100ml (3½oz) Pommeau (French apple brandy)
ice cubes
750ml (25oz) dry cider, well chilled

Pour the lemon juice, sugar syrup and Pommeau into a large bowl. Fill with ice cubes. Stir with a bar spoon until chilled. When ready to serve, finish by adding the well-chilled dry cider.

SPARKLING BRETON PUNCH

MAKES 10

150ml (5oz) freshly squeezed lemon juice
50ml (1⅔oz) sugar cane syrup
250ml (9oz) chouchen liqueur (fermented honey drink similar to mead)
ice cubes
750ml (25oz) dry cider, well chilled

Pour the lemon juice, sugar cane syrup and chouchen liqueur into a large bowl. Fill with ice cubes. Stir with a bar spoon until chilled. When ready to serve, finish by adding the well-chilled dry cider.

OTHER SPIRITS

BELLA SPRITZ

MAKES 1

20ml ($^{2}/_{3}$oz) lavender flower water
60ml (2oz) Aperol®
100ml ($3^{1}/_{2}$oz) Prosecco
30ml (1oz) bitter lemon
ice cubes

TO DECORATE

1 lavender sprig (optional)
$^{1}/_{2}$ lemon slice

Pour the lavender water, Aperol, Prosecco, and bitter lemon into a wine glass. Fill with ice cubes. Mix and serve decorated with the lavender sprig (if using) and half-slice of lemon.

cocktails AROUND THE WORLD

We could take you on a tour around the world in 80 cocktails but let's focus instead on the key ones, the great international classics that you absolutely need to know about and must try on your travels. These are the most iconic cocktails from a selection of different countries.

France

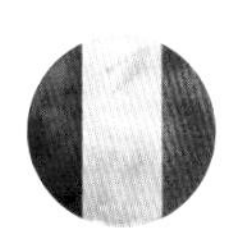

The French are very fortunate to live in a beautiful country with a wine-making tradition. And of course, their rich array of spirits revolves around the vine, which is a huge bonus when it comes to cocktails! However, wine and beer are so deeply embedded in French culture that despite their rise in popularity, cocktails have yet to really compete. It explains why, surprising though it may seem, *kir* is the most widely served and drunk cocktail in France.

KIR CASSIS

MAKES 1

1 part LeJay Lagoute® original crème de cassis
4 parts Bourgogne aligoté white wine, chilled

Pour the crème de cassis into a wine glass and finish by adding the chilled white wine.

Italy

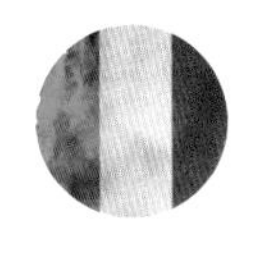

Italy offers a wide range of popular cocktails. It's rich *terroir* and the expertise of Italian producers have made it a celebrated wine-making country. Alongside its excellent vermouths and bitters, Italy also produces Prosecco, a top-quality sparkling wine. So, it is decision time. The sheer number of visitors to Venice each year and of the crowds who flock to Harry's Bar undoubtedly make it Italy's most popular cocktail destination. What do tourists from around the world drink in Harry's Bar, which was opened by Guiseppe Cipriani in 1931? The answer is the famous Bellini, created in 1948. It is still so popular that tourists are already queueing up to sample it as soon as the bar opens. You will have to wait patiently for a seat.

BELLINI

MAKES 1

1 part fresh white peach purée
2 parts Cipriani® Prosecco, chilled

Pour the peach purée into a small ice-cold tumbler and then add the Prosecco. Stir until evenly mixed.

Spain

Synonymous with fiestas and nightlife, Spain owes its night-owl reputation to its warm climate, which is ideal for bars with outside terraces. Like much of Europe, the country has numerous vineyards and the Spanish offer a wealth of local specialities. Strangely, however, on your next visit Spain do not expect to be drinking sangria. For the past ten years or so the Spanish have invited you to try a cocktail that came directly from England. This is Gin and Tonic with a twist, served in a copa-style balloon glass and ice cubes that are a particular size, something each establishment has to order carefully or run the risk of customers in the know refusing the drink. In addition to its special ice cubes, this 'basic' cocktail has been enhanced to produce a flavour explosion on the palate. Each gin goes through a rigorous selection process and bartenders always choose the most appropriate tonic. The final touch is a botanical one, with each mix being served decorated with herbs that highlight the organoleptic qualities of the gin and tonic pairing.

GIN MARE TONIC

MAKES 1

50ml (1⅔oz) Mare® gin
ice cubes
200ml (7oz) Schweppes® Premium Mixer original tonic and lime
1 rosemary sprig
1 strip lemon zest
1 basil leaf

Chill a copa glass until ice-cold and pour the gin into it. Fill the glass with ice cubes and mix gently with a bar spoon. Finish with the tonic and lime and serve decorated with a rosemary sprig, strip of lemon zest and a basil leaf.

United Kingdom

While in Scotland whisky reigns supreme, in England the ruling spirit is gin. In addition to a traditional Gin & Tonic, the English love a Pimm's Cup, a sophisticated cocktail with a true home-grown flavour. Each summer the drink gains in popularity at events on the social calendar such as the Wimbledon tennis tournament, Glyndebourne's opera festival or the Henley Royal Regatta. A number of variations exist, allowing it to be appreciated by as many people as possible. Pimm's No 1 can be served topped up with lemonade, ginger ale, soda water or champagne and decorated with a host of seasonal fruits, citrus fruits, mint or cucumber, all of which deliver a very pleasant taste and olfactory identity.

PIMM'S CUP

MAKES 1

60ml (2oz) Pimm's® No 1
ice cubes
90ml (3oz) lemonade, ginger ale, club soda, or champagne
seasonal fruits
1 slice citrus fruit
1 mint sprig
1 cucumber slice

Pour the Pimm's No 1 into a tall glass. Add ice cubes and then dilute with your chosen mixer. Stir gently and add seasonal fruits, a slice of citrus fruit, a mint sprig and cucumber slice as decoration.

USA

How do you choose the USA's most iconic cocktail? America was the birthplace of the cocktail and many of the world's leading recipes originated there. Taking this as a starting point, it is easy to justify paying tribute to one of the country's oldest recipes, served in prodigious quantities at the annual Kentucky Derby held on the first Saturday in May. During the course of two days' racing, this adds up to some 120,000 mint juleps!

MINT JULEP

MAKES 1

12 mint leaves, plus extra to decorate
25ml (⅔oz plus 1 tsp) sugar syrup
3 dashes Angostura® bitters
80ml (2⅔oz) Kentucky bourbon
crushed ice
icing sugar, to decorate

Place the mint leaves, sugar syrup, bitters and half the bourbon in a silver mint julep cup. Add crushed ice and mix well. The crushed ice must not only cool the cocktail but also dilute it sufficiently to give it the necessary balance. Add the rest of the bourbon, top up with more crushed ice, then mix again. Decorate with an eye-catching dome of crushed ice and a small bunch of mint dusted with icing sugar. Serve with a julep strainer or a straw.

Mexico

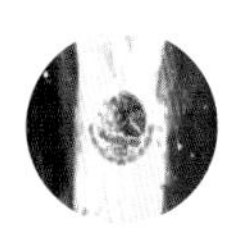

The country of mezcal and tequila overflows with local specialities, including *pulque*, a fermented agave wine that was enjoyed by pre-Hispanic civilizations. Today, everyone dreams of a good Margarita even before they have finished packing their suitcase. However emblematic of the country this cocktail is, its origins remain rather vague with several bartenders claiming the original recipe as their own. It would appear that a woman created it. Madame Margarita Sames came up with the idea of serving her guests a drink made of tequila, triple sec and lime juice. The guests were delighted and reportedly gave the cocktail their hostess's Christian name.

MARGARITA

MAKES 1

lemon juice
table salt
50ml (1⅔oz) tequila
30ml (1oz) triple sec liqueur
20ml (⅔oz) freshly squeezed lime juice
ice cubes

Frost three-quarters of the rim of a cocktail glass with the salt. Do this by pressing the rim in lemon juice and then in salt, covering only three quarters so the drinker has the choice of enjoying the cocktail with or without salt. Pour the tequila, triple sec and lime juice into a cocktail shaker filled three-quarters full with ice cubes. Close it and shake for 10 seconds, then strain into the cocktail glass.

Argentina

One country that really stands out from the crowd when it comes to drinking cocktails is Argentina. When Italian immigrants arrived in the country, they brought with them a speciality from their homeland and turned the Argentinians into enthusiastic consumers of Fernet Branca. This Italian drink, made from herbal bitters with digestive benefits, is not drunk neat in Argentina but mixed with cola to become a Fernet Con Coca, and enjoyed as an aperitif.

FERNET COLA

MAKES 1

60ml (2oz) Fernet Branca®
ice cubes
90ml (3oz) Coca-Cola®

Pour the Fernet Branca into a tumbler. Add ice cubes and then finish by pouring in the cola.

Cuba

When you are in Cuba, deciding between a Mojito, a Daïquiri, a Cuba Libre or a Canchanchara is no easy task. It becomes even more of a challenge in Havana where the influence of these cocktails really makes itself known. Every time of day has its own cocktail and each bar its own speciality. If we had to choose just one, it would have to be the Mojito, a cocktail so revered by the world and yet so hated by the bartending community, which has had to make so many during the course of their careers. Such is the flip side of the celebrity coin. Instead, let's nominate the Daïquiri our iconic cocktail. It first came to prominence in 1898 in the east of Cuba at an iron mine called 'Daïquiri'.

DAÏQUIRI

MAKES 1

50ml (1⅔oz) Bacardi® Carta Blanca rum
25ml (⅔oz plus 1 tsp) freshly squeezed lime juice
1 teaspoon icing sugar
crushed ice and ice cubes

Pour the rum and lime juice into a cocktail shaker and add the icing sugar. Fill the shaker three-quarters full with equal quantities of crushed ice and ice cubes. Close it and shake energetically for 10 seconds, then strain into a cocktail glass.

OTHER SPIRITS

ROSIE SPRITZ

MAKES 1

100ml ($3^1/_2$oz) Italian rosé wine infused with rosebuds (*see* Note)
30ml (1oz) freshly squeezed grapefruit juice
100ml ($3^1/_2$oz) Prosecco
40ml ($1^1/_3$oz) lemonade
ice cubes

TO DECORATE

grapefruit zest (optional)

Pour the rosé wine, grapefruit juice, Prosecco and lemonade into a wine glass. Fill with ice cubes. Mix and add grapefruit zest as decoration.

Note

To prepare the rosé wine infused with rosebuds, place 15–20 rosebuds in a bottle of rosé wine and leave to infuse in the refrigerator for about 24 hours.

OTHER SPIRITS

GREEN FAIRY

MAKES 1

30ml (1oz) orgeat (almond) syrup
30ml (1oz) freshly squeezed lime juice
30ml (1oz) absinthe
ice cubes
30ml (1oz) soda water
1/4 cucumber

Pour all the ingredients, except the soda water and cucumber, into a cocktail shaker. Fill with ice cubes. Shake for about 10 seconds and then pour into an attractive glass filled with ice cubes. Finish with the soda water. Cut the cucumber into thin slices and add to the glass.

OTHER SPIRITS

ITALIAN DREAM

MAKES 1

ice cubes
120ml (4oz) rosé wine
100ml ($3\frac{1}{2}$oz) artisan lemonade
2 raspberries

Fill a balloon wine glass with ice cubes and pour in the rosé wine. Finish with the lemonade and add the raspberries.

OTHER SPIRITS

KYOTO SAKE PUNCH

MAKES 4.5 LITRES (152OZ)

1.5 liters (51oz) sake
900ml (30oz) freshly squeezed grapefruit juice
1.35 liters (46oz) freshly squeezed lemon juice
10 drops of green Tabasco®
450ml (16oz) agave syrup
ice cubes
1 grapefruit
1 lemon

Pour all the liquid ingredients into a cocktail fountain. Mix then add some ice cubes. Cut the grapefruit and lemon into slices and add them to the cocktail fountain. Mix again.

ALCOHOL-FREE

THE *cocktails*

THE EFFECT OF *alcohol-free* AND SPIRIT-FREE

Some bartenders still turn their nose up at non-alcoholic cocktails, and consumers often consider them not worth the bother or even pointless or simplistic. Also known as virgin cocktails or mocktails, alcohol-free cocktails have had a rather rough ride until now, but the democratization of so-called 'advanced' bar techniques on the international cocktail scene has changed this. Far from being simply blended fruit juices or classic cocktails minus the spirits, the new trend is to create drinks that are as interesting, from a technical and flavour point of view, as their cocktail cousins, if not more so.

Extracts, macerations or plant and herb infusions add a significant aromatic richness to a drink and homemade additions like syrups, sweet or tart shrubs, sherbet or a cordial bring originality and a unique flavour. The fact that it is possible to distil a non-alcoholic product also adds an element of surprise both in the technique and the end result.

This alcohol-free trend is beginning to take hold as illustrated by the different 'cocktail weeks' held each year offering, alongside an alcoholic cocktail, a signature non-alcoholic one created by each participating establishment. Today there is no prejudice attached to ordering a non-alcoholic drink, from its very name through to the end result via its decoration. Your mocktail is a fine match for a cocktail.

The mocktail is dead, long live the Spirit-free!

ALCOHOL-FREE

FRESH GREEN TEA

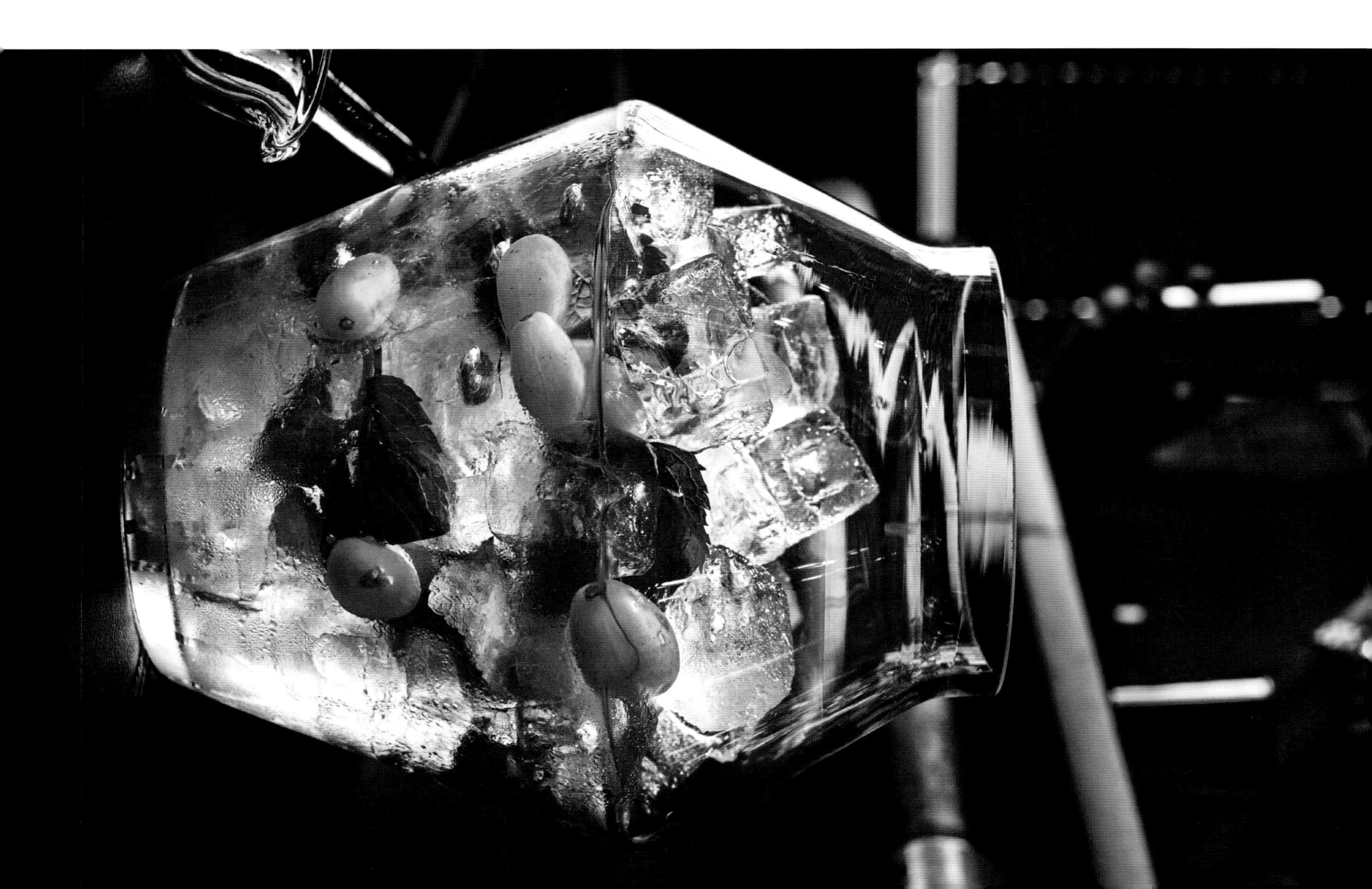

MAKES 10

1 litre (34oz) cold green tea
3 limes
6 mint sprigs
100ml (3½oz) birch sap syrup
200ml (7oz) white grape juice
ice cubes
1 bunch of white grapes

Make the 1 litre (34oz) green tea, leaving it to infuse for 4 minutes at 75°C (167°F). Then leave it to cool completely. Cut 1 lime into slices and juice the other two. Roughly chop the mint. Place the lime slices, lime juice and mint in a large bowl. Pour in the birch sap syrup and white grape juice. Add ice cubes and stir. Finally add the cold green tea. Pick the grapes off their stalks and add to the bowl. Stir again and serve by ladling into attractive glasses.

ALCOHOL-FREE

DIABLOTINI

MAKES 1

50ml ($1^{2}/_{3}$oz) red pepper juice (*see* Note on page 154)
50ml ($1^{2}/_{3}$oz) strawberry juice
10ml (2 tsp) spiced syrup (Spicy de Monin®)
ice cubes
artisan lemonade, to finish

TO DECORATE

2 bird's-eye chillies

Pour the red pepper juice, strawberry juice and spiced syrup into a cocktail shaker. Fill the shaker with ice cubes and shake energetically. Strain into a decorative glass. Finish with a dash of artisan lemonade. Decorate with 2 bird's-eye chillies placed on opposite sides of the glass to resemble the horns of a little devil.

PUSSY FOOT JOHNSON

MAKES 1

1 egg yolk
30ml (1oz) freshly squeezed lemon juice
90ml (3oz) freshly squeezed orange juice
ice cubes
10ml (2 tsp) grenadine syrup

Place the egg yolk, lemon juice and orange juice in a cocktail shaker. Fill the shaker with ice cubes and shake energetically. Strain into a tumbler filled with ice cubes. Finish by adding the grenadine syrup.

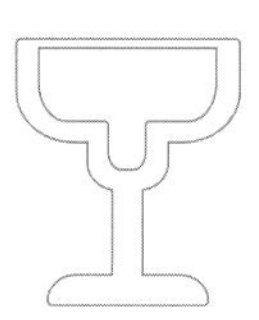

ALCOHOL-FREE

JARDIN DE MAJORELLE

MAKES 1

60ml (2oz) fresh mint green tea
5ml (1 tsp) rosewater
5ml (1 tsp) orange flower water
20ml (⅔oz) sugar cane syrup
shelled pistachios
1 tsp pine kernels

Make the tea in a teapot and add the rosewater, orange flower water and sugar cane syrup. Place the shelled pistachios and pine kernels in a heatproof glass, followed by the tea.

ALCOHOL-FREE

COLOURS

A riot of colours and flavours that will delight everyone from the youngest to the oldest!

MAKES 1

20ml (2/3oz) raspberry syrup
100ml (3½oz) banana juice
ice cubes
100ml (3½oz) strawberry juice

Pour the raspberry syrup into an attractive glass and slowly add the banana juice. Fill the glass with ice cubes, then slowly pour in the strawberry juice.

SPECIAL ICED TEA

What could be more thirst-quenching than high-quality tea made at home and served cold? Bring variety by adding different flavoured syrups. Leave the tea to brew for the desired time, wait for it to cool completely and enjoy!

MAKES 1

1 sachet of Tibetan Monks tea (Palais des Thés®)
20ml (2/3oz) peach syrup (or vanilla, depending on your preference)
lemon and orange zest

TO DECORATE

strips of citrus zest

Following the time indicated on the sachet, infuse the tea in 200ml (7oz) boiling water. Leave it to cool completely. Once the tea is cold, sweeten it with the peach syrup. Add some strips of lemon and orange zest to the tea to boost its flavour. Serve chilled in an attractive glass filled with ice cubes and decorated with strips of citrus zest.

ALCOHOL-FREE

DAISY DELIGHT

Pour the cucumber juice and lychee juice into a wine glass. Fill the glass with ice cubes and stir using a bar spoon. Finish by topping up with lemonade and stir again. Decorate with cucumber or lychee slices and serve well chilled.

MAKES 1

30ml (1oz) cucumber juice (*see* Note)
30ml (1oz) lychee juice
ice cubes
artisan lemonade, to finish

TO DECORATE

cucumber or lychee slices

Note

To make cucumber juice, use a centrifugal juicer or liquidizer. Thoroughly wash the cucumber. Using a vegetable peeler, half-peel by removing strips of skin, leaving alternate strips between with the skin on. Cut the cucumber into dice and put them through a juicer or blend in a liquidizer with a little mineral water, then strain through a conical strainer.

RED LIGHT

MAKES 1

80ml (2⅔oz) raspberry juice
80ml (2⅔oz) strawberry juice
20ml (⅔oz) blackcurrant syrup
70g (2½oz) natural yogurt
ice cubes

TO DECORATE

strawberry slices

Pour the raspberry juice, strawberry juice, blackcurrant syrup and yogurt into a liquidizer. Fill the liquidizer with ice cubes and blend for 10 seconds. Serve in an attractive glass, decorated with strawberry slices. Finish with a stirrer and a straw.

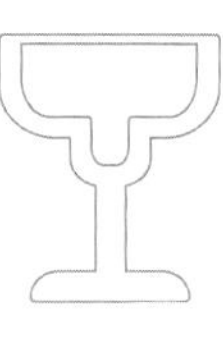

ALCOHOL-FREE

LA BELLE OTERO

MAKES 1

20ml ($^2/_3$oz) elderflower cordial
20ml ($^2/_3$oz) raspberry purée
40ml ($1^1/_3$oz) cold jasmine tea
40ml ($1^1/_3$oz) cranberry juice
ice cubes

TO DECORATE

1 small bunch of redcurrrants

Pour the elderflower cordial, raspberry purée, cold jasmine tea and cranberry juice into a cocktail shaker filled with ice cubes. Shake energetically and strain into a wine glass filled with ice cubes.

Note

Elderflower cordial has a more subtle flavour than traditional syrup, and is more like a concentrated juice with natural aromas and flavours of fruits and spices. Alternatively, try making a variation of the drink using ginger syrup.

ALCOHOL-FREE

FANCY HOT CHOCOLATE

MAKES 1

120ml (4oz) pouring cream
2 × 30g (1oz) bars dark Van Houten® chocolate
150ml (5oz) full-fat milk
1 tablespoon crème fraîche

TO DECORATE

chocolate sprinkles

Pour the cream into a whipping siphon and fit it with two gas cartridges. Turn the siphon up and down to allow the gas to circulate. Store the siphon in the refrigerator for 24 hours. Chop the chocolate and melt it in a small saucepan over a gentle heat. Add the milk and crème fraîche and heat until almost boiling, stirring until smooth. Pour into a cup or heatproof glass and top with a swirl of whipped cream. Decorate with chocolate sprinkles.

NEXT STEP

MAKES 1

120ml (4oz) pouring cream
80ml (2⅔oz) hot Ethiopian coffee
20ml (⅔oz) cinnamon syrup

TO DECORATE

fine strips of orange rind or
1 cinnamon stick

Whip the cream in a siphon, or in a bowl using a stand mixer or a hand-held mixer with a whisk attachment. Store in the refrigerator for 24 hours. Prepare the coffee, pour it into a heatproof glass and add the cinnamon syrup. Top with whipped cream and decorate with fine strips of orange rind or a cinnamon stick.

ALCOHOL-FREE

JULIANA

MAKES 1

40ml (1⅓oz) passion fruit juice
40ml (1⅓oz) peach juice
40ml (1⅓oz) orange juice
10ml (2 tsp) cinnamon syrup
ice cubes

TO DECORATE

½ passion fruit or 1 cinnamon stick

Pour the passion fruit juice, peach juice, orange juice and cinnamon syrup into a liquidizer or cocktail shaker and add some ice cubes. Blend or close the shaker and shake vigorously. Pour into an attractive glass and decorate with the passion fruit half or a cinnamon stick. Serve with a stirrer.

TIKKA ONE

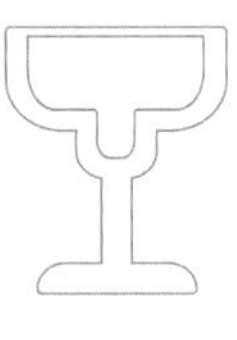

MAKES 1

80ml (2⅔oz) apricot juice
80ml (2⅔oz) pear juice
20ml (⅔oz) pistachio syrup
70g (2½oz) natural yogurt
ice cubes

TO DECORATE

thin pear slices

Pour the apricot juice, pear juice and pistachio syrup into a liquidizer and add the yogurt. Fill the liquidizer with some ice cubes. Blend and then pour into an attractive glass. Decorate with thin slices of pear arranged like a fan. Serve with a stirrer.

ALCOHOL-FREE

PRETTY MAMA

Who doesn't carry the sweet fragrance of their mother close to their heart? This cocktail is dedicated to our mothers!

MAKES 1

30ml (1oz) apple juice
30ml (1oz) apricot juice
30ml (1oz) orange juice
30ml (1oz) pineapple juice
10ml (2 tsp) peach syrup
ice cubes

TO DECORATE

1 wedge of apple or peach

Pour the apple juice, apricot juice, orange juice, pineapple juice and peach syrup into a liquidizer or cocktail shaker. Add some ice cubes and blend or close the shaker and shake vigorously. Pour into an attractive glass. Decorate as you wish with either a wedge of apple or peach. Serve with a straw.

ALCOHOL-FREE

HINT OF VANILLA

MAKES 1

12 mint leaves
4 grapefruit cubes
30ml (1oz) vanilla syrup (or vanilla sugar)
ice cubes
tonic water, to finish

TO DECORATE

1 mint sprig
1 thin slice of grapefruit

Crush the mint leaves, grapefruit cubes and vanilla syrup (or vanilla sugar) in an attractive glass using a muddling tool. Fill the glass with ice cubes. Finish by topping up with tonic water. Serve decorated with a mint sprig and a thin slice of grapefruit. Serve with two straws.

SAN ITALIA

MAKES 1

½ orange slice
ice cubes
120ml (4oz) San Bitter®
60ml (2oz) freshly squeezed grapefruit juice
30ml (1oz) fizzy water (Perrier® or similar)

Place the orange slice in a wine glass filled with ice cubes. Pour in the other ingredients and mix.

ALCOHOL-FREE

WHAT?

MAKES 4

350ml (12oz) rooibos
ice cubes
200ml (7oz) cherry juice
120ml (4oz) freshly squeezed lime juice
120ml (4oz) hibiscus syrup

Make the rooibos infusion, leave it to cool and then chill it in the refrigerator. Half-fill a cocktail shaker with ice cubes, pour in the cherry juice and lime juice. Add the rooibos infusion and hibiscus syrup, close the shaker and shake. Pour into glasses through a strainer.

ALOE SI

MAKES 4

ice cubes
400ml (14oz) aloe Si juice (Caraïbos®)
280ml (9½oz) coconut water
120ml (4oz) Curaçao syrup

Half-fill a cocktail shaker with ice cubes, pour in the aloe Si juice and add the coconut water and Curaçao syrup. Close the shaker and shake for about 10 seconds. Pour into glasses through a strainer.

ALCOHOL-FREE

VEGETITO

MAKES 10

1 kiwi fruit
½ cucumber
1 Granny Smith apple
½ celery stick
1 lemongrass stalk
200ml (7oz) freshly squeezed lime juice
150ml (5oz) sugar syrup
ice cubes
750ml (25oz) raw apple juice

TO DECORATE

1 bunch of mint
cucumber strips
kiwi rounds

Peel the kiwi fruit, cucumber, Granny Smith apple (removing the core as well), celery stick and lemongrass stalk. Cut them into pieces and place in a large bowl. Add the lime juice and sugar syrup with some ice cubes. Mix and add the apple juice. Leave to infuse for several minutes, then serve with ice cubes and straws in large wine glasses decorated with mint sprigs, cucumber strips and kiwi rounds on cocktail sticks.

ALCOHOL-FREE

SUMMER KISS

MAKES 10

1 melon
$^1/_2$ cucumber
150g (1 cup) strawberries
ice cubes
1 litre (34oz) Perrier®

Peel, halve and deseed the melon and the cucumber, then cut into small pieces. Liquidize them in a blender for about 20 seconds. Wash and hull the strawberries and cut each one in half. Place in a large bowl, add ice cubes and pour in the melon and cucumber mixture. Finish by adding the Perrier.

ALCOHOL-FREE

ZEBULON

MAKES 1

½ mango
4 strawberries
100ml (3½oz) pineapple juice
1 coriander sprig
ice cubes

Cut the mango flesh into cubes and halve the strawberries. Place the strawberries and mango in a liquidizer and pour in the pineapple juice. Chop the coriander and add as well. Blend for about 10 seconds, add some ice cubes and blend again for 5 seconds. Pour into a tumbler to serve.

PEACH TALA

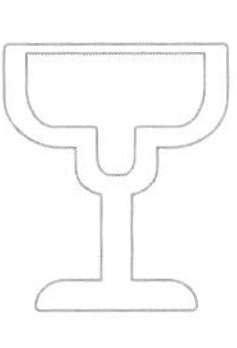

MAKES 1

1 peach
2 apricots
1g (1 pinch) ground turmeric
100ml (3½oz) freshly squeezed orange juice
ice cubes
30ml (1oz) soda water

Peel the peach, remove the stone and cut the flesh into small pieces. Halve and stone the apricots. Place the apricots and peach in a liquidizer. Add the turmeric, orange juice and some ice cubes. Blend for about 10 seconds. Serve in an attractive glass and finish by topping up with the soda water.

ALCOHOL-FREE

VIRGIN COLADA LIGHT

To make this 'light' version, simply replace traditional coconut milk, which is very sweet, with coconut water with no added sugar.

MAKES 1

100ml (3½oz) coconut water (Val Val®)
6 pineapple cubes
10ml (2 tsp) sugar cane syrup

TO DECORATE

desiccated coconut
crushed ice

Pour the coconut water into a liquidizer and add the pineapple cubes and sugar cane syrup. Blend thoroughly. Frost the rim of a tumbler with desiccated coconut and fill with crushed ice. Pour in the blended mixture and serve with straws.

BRAZILIAN

MAKES 1

¼ pineapple
40ml (1⅓oz) maracuja (Brazilian passion fruit) juice
40ml (1⅓oz) freshly squeezed orange juice
ice cubes

Cut the pineapple flesh into 3cm (1¼in) cubes and place in a liquidizer. Add the maracuja juice and orange juice and blend for 10 seconds. To serve, pour into a glass filled with ice cubes.

INDEX BY INGREDIENTS

M

UK/US GLOSSARY OF TERMS

UK	US
beetroot	beet
candy floss	cotton candy
coriander	cilantro
cornflour	cornstarch
courgette	zucchini
crisps	chips
icing sugar	powdered sugar/ confectioners' sugar
kitchen paper	paper towels
lemonade	carbonated lemonade drink (7-Up or Sprite)
plain flour	all-purpose flour
punnet	small basket
prawn	shrimp
single cream/ pouring cream	half and half
vanilla pod	vanilla beans

hamlyn

First published in Great Britain in 2024 by Hamlyn
an imprint of Octopus Publishing Group Ltd
Carmelite House
50 Victoria Embankment
London EC4Y 0DZ
www.octopusbooks.co.uk

An Hachette UK Company
www.hachette.co.uk

Originally published in France by Éditions Larousse in 2019.

Distributed in the US by Hachette Book Group
1290 Avenue of the Americas, 4th and 5th Floors
New York, NY 10104

Distributed in Canada by Canadian Manda Group
664 Annette St, Toronto, Ontario, Canada M6S 2C8

ISBN 978-0-600-63853-7

A CIP catalogue record for this book is available from the British Library.

Printed and bound in China.

10 9 8 7 6 5 4 3 2 1

Hamlyn (English) edition 2024
Editorial Director: Natalie Bradley
Creative Director: Jonathan Christie
Translation: JMS Books LLP and Wendy Sweetser
Senior Editor: Leanne Bryan
Designer: Jeremy Tilston www.theoakstudio.co.uk
Production Manager: Caroline Alberti

Editions Larousse (French) edition 2019
Publishers: Isabelle Jeuge-Maynart and Ghislaine Stora
Editorial Director: Émilie Franc
Editorial Team: Alice Dauphin and Alice Delbarre, assisted by Claire Royo
Graphic Design: Aurore Elie
Layout Design: Lucile Jouret
Production: Émilie Latour

Recipe credits
Pauline Dubois: p. 232–235; Guillaume Guerbois: p. 16, 20, 22, 33, 40, 44, 48, 57, 61, 63, 65, 73, 78, 101, 102, 104, 107, 110, 128a, 131, 138, 146b, 153, 156, 162, 165, 166, 174, 178, 180, 183, 185, 194, 199, 200, 203, 204, 207, 208, 211, 212, 214, 217, 225, 236, 246, 274, 283, 285, 288, 292, 296, 310, 317, 339, 340; Sandrine Houdré-Grégoire: p. 27, 31, 36, 42, 46b, 50, 52, 58b, 74, 88b, 89, 91, 94, 96, 99, 108, 112, 115, 128b, 132b, 134, 136, 141, 146a, 150, 158, 160, 173, 222, 229, 244, 251, 264, 266, 280, 286a, 294, 299, 305, 306, 309, 320, 328, 336, 344b; Sandrine Houdré-Grégoire and Matthias Giroud: p. 18, 24, 28, 29, 34, 39, 46a, 58a, 66, 76, 80, 82, 84, 86, 88a, 97, 116, 123, 124, 126, 127, 132a, 142, 148, 154, 176, 186, 188, 196, 226, 230, 238, 241, 248, 252, 254, 256, 261, 262, 268, 270, 272, 286b, 290, 318, 322, 324, 326, 330, 332, 334, 342, 344a.

Photography credits
© Fabrice Besse: p. 17, 21, 23, 32, 41, 45, 47, 49, 56, 79, 90, 95, 99, 103, 114, 135, 164, 228, 245, 281, 284, 293, 295, 298, 304, 307, 311, 343; © Charly Deslandes: p. 8, 26, 30, 37, 43, 51, 53, 60, 62, 64, 72, 89, 100, 105, 106, 109, 111, 113, 129, 130, 137, 139, 140, 146, 151, 152, 157, 159, 161, 163, 167, 175, 179, 181, 182, 184, 195, 198, 201, 202, 205, 206, 209, 210, 213, 215, 216, 223, 224, 237, 247, 250, 265, 267, 275, 282, 289, 297, 308, 316, 321, 329, 337, 338, 341; © Loran Dhérines: p. 25, 38, 75, 117, 127, 143, 187, 227, 255, 260, 271, 273; © Jean-Blaise Hall: p. 67; © Marie-José Jarry: p. 19, 35, 59, 77, 81, 87, 96, 122, 125, 149, 155, 177, 240, 269, 287, 291, 344; © Olivier Ploton: p. 83, 85, 133, 172, 189, 197, 231, 239, 249, 253, 257, 263, 319, 323, 325, 327, 331, 333, 335; © Shutterstock: p. 10, 11, 14, 54, 55, 70, 120, 170, 220, 242–243, 278, 314; © Fabrice Veigas: p. 232–235.

Illustration credits
Shutterstock: p. 70, Bertrand Loquet : 92–93, iconfree p. 144–145, 258–259, 300–303.